Get Your Head Out of the Clouds, This is Business

Ivy N. McQuain

Published by BLI Publishing, a subsidiary company of The BLI Group, Dallas, TX.

CreateSpace.

Printed in the United States of America.

Designed by BLI Solutions, a subsidiary of The BLI Group, Dallas, TX.

ISBN-13: 978-0615786315
ISBN-10: 0615786316

DEDICATION

I dedicate this book to you. The business owner who doesn't know which way is up but they believe they have a purpose and were called to do what they do. Good luck to you.

Contents

ACKNOWLEDGMENTS

My first thank you is to God for His loving mercy and His push to get me off my behind to write this book. Then I want to thank Jesus for loving me even though I fought with Him constantly. Next, I want to thank and apologize to my two sons, Demerial and Nickohlas. I am sorry that it took us to lose everything more than just once to get me to write this darn book. Ridiculous. Now I completed what you two have been waiting on me to complete so thank you for being there.

Thanks to my mom for everything. It was her consistent nagging that made me say, "I can't stay with her," so I wrote this book. (SMILE). Thanks to my friends, especially Ebony Holmes, for encouraging me and saying, "That sounds good." And the rest of the SKILLED women, thank you. Thank you to my clients for the experience. Thank you Eric Bettis, my business partner, for putting up with me. Love you all.

Chapter ONE

YOU

All my life I loved writing and when I wasn't writing I thought about it. So much so, that I had books already written – this being one of them. I had titles for other books, characters, plots … the whole nine yards ready to go but I wasn't. I can only imagine how many words I've wasted in useless emails and social media posts as I let my destiny hang out in journals, on my laptop and on loose pieces of paper. I mean I wrote all the time – articles, business writings for various client, applications, emails, anything to keep my fingers moving and my brain going. But I couldn't make time to write for myself … to get my head out of the clouds so God could bless me.

But God has a way to light a fire inside you and under your feet that not even you can put out. For me it happened while I was doing my usual routine, going on Facebook and liking people's status or reposting interesting things that my 'friends' would possibly like. I came across the Quit2Write contest, sponsored by *Simply Beautiful Magazine* and thought, 'sure why not.' I only entered the contest because I was frustrated with not having money to take care of my boys. I was mad at myself for having a God given talent that I was taking for granted.

I won the contest and received an autographed copy of Nakia Laushal's book *Running from Solace*. I also won a 30-minute consultation with Laushal that lasted for almost an hour. Laushal, a Houston resident, was shocked and utterly appalled that I had already completed not only one book but two books and was refusing to publish them. And she let me have it. She told me that she felt no sympathy for me and that I deserved to be in the condition I was in because I wasn't being obedient to my calling. She was frustrated with me but talked to me like I was her friend. She encouraged me to publish this book even if it was only for my eyes.

I smiled at that idea because I honestly didn't want people to judge my writing permanently. Now keep in mind that I have been a professionally published writer since 1998. I may have written thousands of articles in various magazines, newspapers, and online sites across the world, some that have been used in noted publications. I even host *The Executive Corner*, an Internet based show that I self-produce and direct. So I have no problems with words, at least in the short run like articles.

Talk about a ridiculous fear. I now look back at how many years I wasted arguing with people who believed in my abilities. I now know that God allowed me to be delayed until I was mentally ready to handle the realization of where I put myself. That made me determined to succeed because it was my fault that I lived in lack despite having a business and being a published writer for my entire adult life.

To this day I thank Laushal for telling me something that brought tears to my eyes. She said, "When my son saw me complete my first book, he started to want to be successful and do more with himself." My answer to her now is that I hope my sons will look at me completing this book as an opportunity for them to do better and to accomplish their dreams without delay.

Our delay, be it financial, emotional or spiritual, was my fault because I refused to be successful on God's terms. I wanted nothing more than the short-term gratification of writing an article and moving on to the next topic. So I had to finish this book as an apology to my sons. I had to apologize to them for taking my talents and God for granted.

Now it's your turn to get out of your own way. You have had just as many excuses as I have had, maybe more, maybe less but it doesn't matter because at the end of the day you are still in the same boat of half stepping, complaining and downright sitting on your butt. More than likely you're still frustrated with your circumstances in some way. You whine about your business, cry about your bills, yell at your family because of you. You refuse to get your head out of the clouds about owning a business. It's your time now.

You want to be a business owner? But you can't because you don't delay what you need to do to become a successful business owner. You delay educating yourself about business, your trade, and its industry. You delay honing your craft. You delay managing and investing your money for your business correctly. You can't and won't succeed in business because you are constantly delaying yourself. So it's time that you stop daydreaming about being successful and start making success a reality.

This book, *Get Your Head Out of the Clouds, This is Business*, is my no nonsense approach to business. It's a compilation of articles, in their raw form, that I have written over the years that my readers felt were beneficial. It's also about my experiences over the years as a business owner. The articles I selected are not only helpful but offer good old fashion kick in the butt advice, that we all need from time to time.

I have to be upfront and warn you now … this book will not be filled with unicorns and butterflies that give you delusions of grandeur. No, I will deliver unfiltered advice like Laushal gave to me on October 5, 2012 at 11:00 a.m. CST. She didn't feel sorry for me and I refuse to feel sorry for you, especially when God gave you your talents to share with the world. It's time to stop the pity party song and dance because at the end of the day it's your fault why you kept delaying being successful as a business owner. I'm here to tell you what it really takes to be successful in business, so grab a notebook and pen, sit down and let the words on these pages soak in.

Are YOU a Leader?

"Before you embark upon any endeavor research, research, research."

I live by these words. Sometimes loosely and other times I make sure I know everything there is to know about new opportunities presented to me. I research every opportunity, not only for the financial benefits but to know if the opportunity will develop me as a leader as well as my talents. So I offer you this advice, as you research, whatever it maybe, get to know who you are as a leader first.

When trying to understand leadership you can enroll in any management or psychology class. The will tell you about the different types of leadership styles, which include laissez-faire, autocratic, participative, transactional and transformational. I could go into detail about these leadership styles but Google will help you better than I can. My goal is to take a different approach based on my personal experience about business. Keep in mind that what I'm about to tell you is what I consider to be leadership traits. These traits are based on my 15 years of entrepreneur experience and may actually fall into one of the official leadership styles. That's why it's important for you to research the above leadership styles so that you know who you are as a leader. I exhibit at least one or more of these traits, from time to time. Some of these traits help me to be a sound leader, while others cause me stress and frustration. Either way it is good to be a well-balanced leader who seeks guidance, is willing to learn and grow, and wants to teach and grow other leaders. If you don't want to help others, then you are definitely headed down the wrong path as a business owner.

You need to know who you are as an individual and what you will, can, will not and cannot tolerate. At some point, you will use all of these traits because as a leader you have your own predetermined wills, cans and nots based on who you are. Basically, that means what you will and will not tolerate. You have to understand the good, bad, and ugly traits that you may possess as a business owner and as a leader, as well as how to use them to make sound business decisions.

THE GOOD

- *The Friend.* This leadership trait is a good trait to have if you want to be an employee because it is the one that does not want to offend people. As the friend you run to everyone's aide hoping they give back to you what you give to them. The friend tends to have fewer boundaries in their business practices because they don't want to upset their customers or employees. You also avoid confrontation, sometimes at all costs.

- *The Doormat.* The doormat trait means that you are prone to being used. You rarely standup for yourself and you prefer to follow rather than lead. Doormats want to say no but do not know how. The friend trait could possibly become the doormat because of the need to help everyone and to be the 'nice guy.' I know I have this under good but it's because this trait possesses the ability to cooperate in most cases.

- *The Helper.* This is a great trait to have but it should not be your primary trait. The helper can easily be taken advantage of because of their desires to help every business owner with a sob story. Most entrepreneurs fall into the helper category when they start off because they think, 'If I help them, then they will help me.' Being a helper shows a commitment to growing other people and fostering lasting relationships.

THE BAD

- *The Know-It-All.* The know-it-all is a trait that makes you think you know everything about everything but in reality you really don't. Having the know-it-all trait will limit your growth because you're less likely to receive advice from people you feel aren't as smart or knowledgeable as you are.

- *The "Bitch".* Don't get offended because we all know one, be they man or woman. The B (to make you feel better) is a both a good and bad trait. Being a B in business means you're not tolerable to things that don't benefit you. It also means possibly running off people who can help you. Balancing this trait is important. In other words, don't tolerate foolishness, but don't run off your help.

- *The Talker.* The talker trait knows how to talk themselves in and out of any situation. Unfortunately, the talker trait can cause you to be short on delivering on what they say they can deliver. Having the talker trait means you agree to things before you fully understand it or you accept opportunities knowing you can't deliver on it. For business owners who are talkers, they tend to make other business owners skeptical of honest business owners because of the deception.

- *The Dictator.* The dictator trait limits you from accepting help. Most of the time a person with a dominate dictator trait has been burnt in business and believes as if they can't trust anyone. Other times the dictator trait shows up in a new business owner who feels as if they have to do everything alone because they can't afford to hire help. Either way the dictator trait is a bad primary trait to have.

THE UGLY

- *The User.* The user trait makes an individual very charismatic and agreeable. But those who possess this trait as a primary trait are keen on getting information or services out of you. The business owner who possesses this trait is self-centered and egotistical and will act as if they did the work they know they didn't complete. Having this as a dominate trait will cause others to distrust you and leave. I am not saying don't seek out information but be someone that gives as well.

- *The Betrayer.* The betrayer trait is what it says, a betrayer. The entrepreneur who uses this trait the most often will leave a trail of broken relationships, burnt bridges, and poor decision making. Business owners who are betrayers arc often envious of others they have worked with; they lie on others to get clients; and they may even steal some of your ideas. They may even be so bold to do steal your ideas while they are still hanging around you. This is the worst trait, next to the user.

I wrote this article, *The connecting climb of a leader*, originally published in *Black MBA* in 2010, the nationally published magazine for the National Black MBA Association. This article received a lot of attention and is based on the teachings of my pastor Pastor Rickie G. Rush of the Inspiring Body of Christ Church in Dallas, TX. What I want you to take away after reading this book is a solid understanding of being a strong leader:

> Are you able to gather your entire staff together or just the star employees who are able to keep up with your leadership style? Do you feel like your employees are not on board with your vision and mission and often find yourself frustrated and disappointed by the quality of employees you have? You may find it frustrating when attempting to unify your employees. Unfortunately, it may not be your employees but rather you as the leader. Understanding your leadership style is the key to having effective employees who will go the distance for you and make your department goals a reality.
> As a small business owner, I realized that I had to take on multiple personalities to sustain my business.
> Specifically, by being a climber and a connector I would make my business thrive through various economic conditions. As a climber, I instinctively think about

positioning my business for success. I wanted to move upwards and increase business, which made me aware of my competition's position, regardless if they were behind or in front of me. I also have the personality of a connector, because I focus on relationships that have caused me brief moments of stagnation. I have focused on clients who were not motivated to attain the next level of their business.

As I move forward as a small business owner, I have had to learn to balance my personalities to ensure success for my business and those involved. If your climber personality is dominating and you want to sustain relationships with your employees without losing your focus on upward mobility for your team, you should:

Show appreciation for your employees. I had to learn to show appreciation for those involved in my organization. By showing appreciation, you acknowledge the differences among your employees and let them know you care about what they add to your team.

Be sensitive to your employees. As a climber, I had a no nonsense policy when dealing with my team and clients. I had to learn that being sensitive to my employees adjusted their mood and helped me understand how they felt. If your employees have a problem expressing themselves or if they over express themselves, your sensitivity will help bridge communication issues.

Stay consistent. I strive for consistency in every aspect of business by being effective, honest and open, not fake or forced when I address concerns or give compliments. Employees do not like inconsistencies because inconsistencies show that a leader is not effective.

Know who you are. I thought that as a small business owner I had to be the top dog all the time, but I soon realized it was not a loss if my employees or clients won. If you have a shining star on your team, it is important you celebrate their win. Insecurities of your employees winning can hurt your team's morale.

Know that it's OK to laugh. I laugh all the time as a business owner but I am serious when it comes to ensuring my clients and employees are taken care of. As a leader, you do not have to excessively joke with them but being able to laugh with your employees and use humor, even if you are not funny, makes a connection.

If your leadership personality is to connect rather than climb and you are ready to unify your employees through advancement, you should:

Increase your energy. I have been drained as a small business owner and lost energy. Increasing my energy increased my productivity. Show your employees you are capable of being an energized leader.

Manage your connections. As a connector, I focused on the relationships that were negative to the development of my business. I learned to end relationships and manage others that did not align with my vision. Manage relationships and focus on valuable connections rather than being known as the "friendly boss".

Intensify your sense of purpose and urgency. There were times when I lacked urgency due to periods of slow business. I had to learn to intensify my sense of purpose on projects and my urgency to show my employees I wanted more for them and my business. As a leader, your intensity sets the tone for your team.

Leaders can develop their skills by finding the right relationships. Let your employees know you want to win, that you believe they can win, that you want to win with them and that when they win, you win, too. Leadership is complicated and being successful as a climber who connects or a connector who climbs will add more to your team.

Which traits do you think you possess? Remember, you can have more than one leadership trait. But if the bad ones outweigh the positive ones, then you may need to reevaluate yourself as a leader.

JUST YOU

Many people fail to identify who they are as an entrepreneur before they dive head first into a business endeavor. They don't realize that they may not be able to handle stressful situations; that they may not be a go-getter or self-starter; or that they just don't have the stamina or endurance to survive clients who don't pay on time or who just won't pay at all.

That's why you need to know who you are first. You need to know your pain tolerance for the heartaches that business ownership will bring you. When I started my first business at 19 years old at Texas Southern University in Houston, I was sure of one thing… I didn't want to be someone's employee for the rest of my life. I knew I had an issue with being told what to do. I had an issue of watching the wrong people succeed. I had an issue with lazy mentality and a lack of pride. So I knew that entrepreneurship was the only path for me. Unfortunately, I didn't know who I was, so I went to work for other people and experienced everything that I didn't like. Why? Because I didn't take the time to find out who I was as a business owner. I got scared of being without that fulltime business ownership would bring me. So many of us do this but it's time to understand that even in your job you can be without so why not do what you love doing and step out on faith?

This book is to help you understand who you are first and foremost as a business owner, before you ever get started in business. I want to encourage you to answer these questions now to gauge yourself as a business owner:

1. Do I know why I want to start a business?
2. Do I want to start my business because I think I can do a better job than someone else?
3. Is there really a need for my services or product?

4. If I start my business will it deal with my calling or gift or my desires to just have a business?
5. What am I willing to sacrifice to make my business grow?
6. Can I honestly sacrifice my personal time, my friend time, my relationship time to be a successful business owner?
7. Am I able to motivate myself when I don't have an audience?

If you already have a business but you wake up every day frustrated, then here are some questions you need to ask yourself to help you identify who you are as a business owner:

1. Why did I start my business in the first place?
2. Am I walking in my calling or using my God given gift to serve others?
3. Did I start my business because I saw someone else doing what I wanted to do?
4. When I started my business did I really do a market analysis to determine if there was a need for my business?
5. Do I really want to keep fighting when things get tough in my business?

Every day people start businesses without first evaluating their ability to be a business owner. They fail to do the necessary research of the business and industry they are trying to enter into. They simply believe that they are talented in some specialized area or they listen to people who don't know what it takes to be a successful entrepreneur. Unfortunately, we all know someone, maybe even ourselves, who got into business because they saw someone else doing what they thought they could do. We have all been a victim of the 'anything you can do I can do better' mentality. But its that mentality that hurt so many business owners and cause businesses to fail.

I can honestly say the one thing that continues to confuse me is how so many people start businesses without any clear direction of where they are going or who they are. They literally don't know how a business works or what it takes to be a business owner. Some think *'I have the money, so why not start a business less than two miles from my competitor?'* While others truly believe that they know enough people who will just throw money at them.

It's both hilarious and frustrating to consult people who want to start a business but know absolutely nothing about it. It boggles my mind how these people have no tolerance when it comes to dealing with clients, employees, vendors or anyone else. I am also clueless as to how these same people seek advice from after 5 entrepreneurs. You know those people who do business after they get off their job? You should always seek advice from people who are where you want to be, not trying to be where you are.

That's why I finally decided to finish this book because you need to know that being a business owner takes real work. You won't get glitter wands and wishing rocks. Nope you'll get headaches. You'll cry rivers. You'll even have multiple homicide, manslaughter and assault cases buried in your mind but if you really have what it takes, you'll keep moving forward and make your business a success.

Here is an excerpt from an article *Ways to hurt your small business* I wrote in 2010 for the *Examiner.com Small Business* section. This article addressed the various ways that entrepreneurs hurt their business.

> Many entrepreneurs fail to understand the value of
> their business and the necessary requirements needed for

growth. They do not take the time to learn the practical applications and requirements to make their business a success, in and far past their targeted market. These entrepreneurs typically have a skewed view of what they need or how they will accomplish growth for their business. The reasons why entrepreneurs fail to value their business are endless but I was able to find some common issues from clients I have encountered and in general brainstorming conversations:

Lack of commitment. When you become an entrepreneur it is like taking a sacred vow to protect, honor and obey the rules and regulations of that business. Oftentimes entrepreneurs fail to commit themselves because of other issues in their lives. They allow trivial situations to interfere and impact the growth and development of their business. They lack the ability to balance their personal lives which causes their commitment to their business to wane. The entrepreneur who always has something more important to do is one that does not need to start a business full-time. Just jump into a direct selling company or do it as a side hustle until your commitment level surpasses your ability to deliver.

I admit that in my 15 years of business experience, I have lacked commitment to my business more than once. I know I should be well beyond what I envisioned for myself, but then you wouldn't have my personal testimony to help you get out of your own way. I challenged everything that had to deal with me waking up and working in my calling. I believed that I needed to work for someone else because of my children. I didn't want to lack but I was living paycheck to paycheck. I hope you understand my experiences and use them to get off of your butt.

I remember meeting the owner of an online jewelry boutique at Barnes and Noble in the Irving Mall in 2010. To this day our initial meeting has left a lasting impression on the both of us. When we met she looked as if she stepped out of a magazine. But what I didn't anticipate was the whining and complaining she did for more than 30 minutes about how she was having her ideas stolen by people she thought she could trust and how she wanted to give up. I immediately knew that she wasn't committed to growing her business, she was committed to complaining and all things negative.

I thought we were meeting to start a business relationship and for her to become my client. Instead it was complaint after complaint so I just closed my business notebook and stared at her. She stopped and asked me what I was doing and I told her that she needed to go and get a 9-5 because she clearly was not committed to growing her business. I offered to redo her resume so she could reenter the workforce. You can imagine how shocked she was, but for me the time I spent listening to her was wasted time. I was upset because I could have been meeting with a prospective client who was committed to growing their business.

When we left, after a few hours, I consulted, counseled and mentored her on how to successfully grow her business. My first piece of advice was to change her attitude about her business. I urged her to get her mind right because she was spending too much time complaining and not enough time working to position her business for success. After our initial meeting, she pulled away almost completely from me but she would call asking a simple question that would sometimes turn into an hour of free advice. I had to tell her that I would start billing for my consulting and then the calls stopped altogether.

In hindsight it's funny because she learned a valuable lesson, don't waste time complaining. Eventually, she recommitted herself to making her business grow. She also admitted that I was one of the meanest but most honest people in business that she had talked to. She said I challenged her to commit to her business rather than committing to complaining and whining about the gift God had given her. So stop whining and start committing.

Are You Really Committed?

Commitment takes dedication, motivation and passion to push forward to become a successful business owner. But don't get confused because while you are refocusing your commitment to your business, you still can hurt your business by jumping on every opportunity someone presents to you. I can't tell you how frustrating it is to look on Facebook or any social media site and see the same person starting a new company or offering a new service without perfecting or honing their initial business concept. I get that it's important to have multiple streams of income but don't be known as a Jack of All Trades But Master of None and too many so-called business owners are known for their ability to offer, but their inability to deliver.

If you are one of these people who always has a new hustle then let me be the first to let you know that you clearly have no real concept of what it takes to grow and build a business. It takes years to perfect one career path, so think about what it takes to perfect being a business owner. McDonalds perfected the Big MAC before it ever thought about the McRib. Get my point? Stick to perfecting one concept long enough to watch it flourish before jumping into a new venture. You have to realize that staying in your lane is essential when committing and growing your business. Always remember, just because you can doesn't mean you should.

Stinking Thinking Be Gone

I have witnessed so many entrepreneurs gripe and complain about clients, prices, heck just about anything. Remember the online boutique owner? She came to the meeting ready to complain about everything and everyone. Do you do that?

Complain all the freaking time about everything, especially if someone is listening? If you do, stop it. You don't need to get everything off of your chest. You are not a 5th grader. You're an adult who made the choice to start a business, so stop the whining.

You can have success beyond your wildest dreams but you, not someone else, can't get past all of the fussing and complaining you do. So what if you shared your idea with someone and they made it happen. That doesn't mean they are going to succeed. That just means you talk too much. And you forgot the cardinal rule… what God has for you is for you! So stop holding yourself hostage with misery and unhappiness that takes control of every aspect of your life and ultimately hurt your business and the relationships you have fostered. Sometimes our ideas are for others to manifest. So instead of complaining that someone stole your idea, thank God that you were obedient to speak it and that someone else is going to be blessed from it … then move the hell on.

Make no mistake about it, I still struggle with complaining, especially when I've done all I can for a client. But guess what? They can't take advantage of me unless I let them. When I find myself fussing I quickly realize that my words will destroy everything that I have prayed for. So I change my speech to reflect the blessings that I know are waiting for me. I know how easy it is to be negative, fuss, and bring mess into every aspect of your life. But I challenge you to change how you talk and take time to distress before you say something you can't take back. I know firsthand what it's like to have a negative business outlook. Nothing made me happy until I lost it all. Until I woke one day living in a motel room with my sons. Talk about a rude awakening. God had blessed me so many times to get it together, but I refused to stop cursing myself with my negative outlook, stinking thinking and the way I talked.

I wrote *Your mouth CAN defeat you* before I ever fully understood the power of my tongue. Again this article is based on the teachings of Pastor Rush:

> Ever heard the saying, "You are what you say?" Well this is a very true statement and as an entrepreneur one you should not take lightly. The reason is simple because you want to succeed and hopefully leave a legacy, also known as your business, to your loved ones. But you can't do that if you are always speaking the negative of being a business owner. It just won't happen.
>
> Just think about what the Bible says about the tongue in James 3:7-9 – *"For every kind of beast and bird, of reptile and sea creature, can be tamed and has been tamed by mankind, but no human being can tame the tongue. It is a restless evil, full of deadly poison. With it we bless our Lord and Father and with it we curse people who are made in the likeness of God."* This one passage should show you that your tongue can garner you a successful business or destroy it. Want to know how? Keep reading but brace yourself because you just might find something you currently do or have done.
>
> When a client upsets you, you immediately make it known to others. Always remember you never know who someone else knows. With that take certain care to never speak ill against a client or potential client in a manner that could be detrimental to the growth of your business. You may think you are venting when you use your social media accounts and tell the events of what happened between you and the client but be assured the world is smaller than you think and the Internet has a stronger and faster memory than you do. If you are upset at something a client did or said, keep it to yourself and use it as a learning tool for another day. Please don't take your grievances to Facebook or Twitter just because you have to "let it be known you are not to be messed with."
>
> You share confidential information although you never mention the person or persons involved. As a business owner you are not on an interview to get a job, you are highlighting your accomplishments and telling a potential client how you will better their business.
>
> "As a seasoned business owner, I am always perplexed how people feel the need to share confidential information

about a client experience just to gain admiration or sympathy from others," says Lara Michelle, owner of Legendary Beauty Salon and Spa and Lara Michelle Cosmetics, a makeup and skincare company for women of color.

Confidential is just that ... confidential. Use successes from an experience, not the negative or the steps and actions or even the resistance.

You relate the hardness of your business. "I had a long day with my clients." "Ugh these clients don't understand what it takes to run a business, LOL." There are so many negatives comments you actually say before you ever get the goodness of being an entrepreneur. Yes, it is important to be honest about your situation but some things should be taken to God first and only God before you share with others. Instead of fixating on the negatives of your work day try making every experience positive. For instance, instead of chastising clients for being hard on you, simply thank God that you have clients and listen to what they have to say. There may actually be an opportunity in the fussing to make improvements to your business.

You count yourself out before you ever get started. One of the easiest things entrepreneurs do is give up before they get started. They ask another entrepreneur for a price quote and because they don't have the budget available they give up on the efforts. Or they refuse to bid on large projects because they think it takes more than what they can give. They speak or think and act on the temporary lack of. Stop doing this if you want to succeed.

You complain and complain and complain and complain. The most disturbing characteristic of an entrepreneur is a complaining one. You are blessed, let's get that out of the way. You have the ability and know how to operate a business. A business you created or acquired but you complain that you stay up late hours; that you have no free time; that your clients are ungrateful; that you are not making the money you should be; that you offer discounts and people still want things free.

Complaints and the one thing that all of these statements have in common, YOU! As an entrepreneur you set your prices, you set your discounts, you determine your clients, you work the hours you need to get the job done. If you are not managing your time or losing money dealing with unscrupulous clients, then that is your fault, not theirs.

> Bottom line … your tongue can cause destruction to your business or it can grow your business. Speak what you desire into existence and then walk in the belief that it is already done.

I was bold enough to advise others about their business and complaining but never listened to my own advice. I gave advice to a now celebrity makeup artist who complained a lot too when she first started her craft. But the one complaint that stuck out to me was about her husband's hesitation to support her. I told her, 'if I had to listen to you complaining all day about the business you say you love, I wouldn't support you either.' She got the point and started to change her perspective and the way she talked about her blessing.

You have to be willing to shed that stinking, putrid, and vile thinking. The Bible says clearly, so a man thinks, he is. Stop wasting time with the negative thoughts about your business. If the people you associate with think and talk negatively all the time, then change the people you hang out with. It doesn't matter who they are, you need to change the negative people you associate with. Even if that means losing a majority of your clients and only having one. Just use that one to rebuild your business and set the standard for who you want as clients.

Personal Life

The final thing that I want to discuss in this chapter is your personal life. You can't succeed if you don't have the tolerance to deal with your personal life. Granted you have a family, children, significant other and other responsibilities but those things should not impede or impact the success of your business. If you balance your personal life with your business life just right, then your business will take care of your obligations, which is your ultimate goal.

A business owner who doesn't know how to function without some level of personal life drama is trouble. They let their drama take their focus away from their business, then they have the audacity to complain. They rush to every personal life crisis, even if it's not a crisis. It seems as if they love dealing with personal life challenges. But that crap don't make them better as a business owner, it makes people not want to deal with them because they know that something distracting is always going to come up.

Let me be clear, it's important to deal with your personal life but everything has a place and time. If your business is your primary income, heck even if it's not, then it's important to keep your personal and business life separate. You wouldn't dare bring your personal life drama to your job without risking getting fired, so why do it to your business? Think about Job from the Bible, though his personal life ended in shambles he never took his eyes off the promises of God. Think of your business as the promise of God, don't lose focus by focusing on unnecessary issues in your personal life. And I know you know what's necessary and unnecessary to deal with.

Businesses can't survive in chaos; therefore your personal life should be in order before you even try to start a business. You can only make sound decisions when you can think and focus clearly. The less stress you have in your personal life, the more capable you are of handling business related issues, rather than pushing them off to focus on personal issues. Always try to figure things out instead of whining, complaining, fussing or avoiding issues all together. After all your business will drain you enough, so you don't need to bring unhandled personal life issues into the mix.

My personal testimony about having to get my personal life together so I could finish what God told me to do deals with me losing everything more than once. I had to stop blaming my ex-husband because he moved on with his life after our divorce. I had to stop blaming the fathers of my sons because my sons are successful without their input. I had to stop blaming my mother, which was something I perfected, because she has always been my biggest cheerleader. I realized that it was my responsibility to get my personal life together so God could use me.

Now, it's time to get your ish together.

For me, God had lit a fire under me and I no longer had time to waste dealing with personal issues especially those that were none of my business. I no longer had time to attend my own pity parties. I'm now determined to use my time to do everything God told me to do. I'm determined to live in obedience and in God's will and design for my life. I'm determined to stop wallowing in the misery of personal chaos that I created for myself. I'm determined to live my best life. That's why you're getting the hard truth about business. Besides I'm allergic to flowers so I can't tiptoe through the tulips to make you feel better.

So what are you going to do to get you ready to become a successful business owner. Start with leaving the drama out of your life, getting your mind right and moving into the vision God has for you.

Get Your Mind Right

At the end of each chapter, I will present a true to life question section to help you understand if you are truly ready to be a business owner. Just be sure to answer in truth and read them as you see fit:

1. Am I resting on my laurels?
2. Do I have an, 'Eh, I'm good at what I do, so there is no need to do more' attitude?
3. Do I allow fear to keep me where I hate being?
4. Have I wanted more but feared rejection outside of my circle of friends and family or even myself?
5. Have I called out to God to help me make a way to provide for my family and myself and all I hear Him say was, 'I already have?'
6. Do I feel a fire inside of me that scares me? A fire so strong that it literally propelled me to get off my butt and do something more?
7. What personal issues are constantly getting in the way of my business?
8. If I let those negative personal issues go in my life, then will my life be better?
9. Can I afford to wait any longer?

Chapter Two

Money

We all know that you can start a business on a relatively small amount of money. The Internet has made sure of that with all of the free options for websites, business cards and marketing and advertising opportunities through social media. Unfortunately, these free options are not the cure all for growing a successful business. They are limited and most startup businesses have these same template designs.

There is a cost for keeping your business afloat and on a growth track for years to come. You have to have a plan that makes sense financially. I'm not one to tell anyone to divert their dreams, but if you can't survive off your business income, then you need to keep your day job until you have the money saved (recommended at least six months to a year) to walk away. The only problem with that is people become complacent at their jobs and their dreams of becoming a fulltime business owner quickly becomes delayed or denied altogether.

You have to have supernatural faith to become a fulltime business owner and to completely trust God. You can always take temp jobs when you need some right now money but for the most part being a business owner is a fulltime gig. You typically get up before everyone else does and go to sleep after everyone. I have been so determined to not work for anyone else anymore that I often work into the wee hours of the morning. I knew that I could earn a better living on my own than for any company. After all being a business owner has earned me more than $10,000 a month, money I knew I would never make at a job.

Despite the financial success, I've had it took ne a long time to become financially committed to growing my business. I struggled to balance each payment I received from my clients, especially when it came to investing in back into my business. I had horrible spending habits and figured that it was easy for me to make money so there was no need to save it. But 2012 proved to be a financially stressful year for me which quickly changed my perspective on how to commit my finances to growing The BLI Group as well as my professional writing career. I now understand that at least 50 percent of my revenue must go back into the company before we ever receive a dime. I had to pay off debt, make purchases for the company and develop a grow, grow, grow mentality.

Before I get started on telling you how to commit financially to your business, let me say this… YOU CANNOT commit to your business financially if you flip flop on your prices like a politician does on the issues. It's not going to happen. Human nature, remember that word, because it kicks in and most people want something for nothing. So you have to know your worth and commit to your prices before you ever get started in business. Being relaxed on your pricing structure will cost you in the long run. So don't overdo it with giving deals, bartering for services, and hooking people up.

So I urge you to set your prices based on your experience, business worth, education and what it costs for you to grow your business. Don't lose sleep over people who can't afford your services because they come a dime a dozen. They'll get over it and you'll grow from it.

Commit Financially

I wrote *Financially committing to your small business*, in 2010. This article advised entrepreneurs on how to commit to their business financially:

> Are you aware that you may be financially ruining your company because you do not understand the importance of financially committing to your business? Yes, but you are not the only one who is not willing to do more for their business because of the 'recession' or because they are just unaware of what it truly takes to take their business to the next level. Fortunately, there are ways to increase your exposure through effective financial commits.
>
> *Financially committing to your advertising/marketing strategy:* Your business may be able to grow or even sustain from word of mouth but you better have the best whatever you are selling or servicing in your market because if you are not willing to advertise/market business your, it will only grow as far as someone's voice will take it. Try business cards, postcards, websites, sponsored events, national or local ad campaigns but do something to maximize your client base.
>
> *Financially committing to your employees:* You cannot expect to hire quality workers for less than the cost of a postage stamp! While I know it may be difficult to pay your employees big bucks but you should do some research to determine the proper pay grade, offer incentives and bonuses and other perks to keep your employees performing at their best.
>
> *Financially committing to your clients/customers:* Without clients/customers you have absolutely no reason to exist as an entrepreneur. Committing your company dollars to show appreciation for your customers, offer discounts, or order quality products is worth the cost to upgrade if you will. Always strive to make your customers feel they are the best ever.

Financially committing to your investors: If you are fortunate to have investors such as family and friends, be sure to pay your them back in a timely manner and keep them current on financial matters and concerns.

Financially committing to yourself: Notice you were last? Well that is because your business should be invested and reinvested in before you even think about hitting the malls to shop. You should have a predetermined salary for yourself and make due with that amount.

Hopes and having your head in the clouds about the financial future of your business will not sustain it. You need consistent money flowing in. The article above definitely helps with identifying valuable ways to commit to your business financially. I have to admit that it irks me to see business owners, who after a few years of being in business, still want to receive free services, want interns, or can't pay their creditors. I mean really, what the heck have they been doing with the money they've been earning from clients? Don't be like these people who just use folks to get ahead. Take the time to invest in your business before you lose it to debt.

Cheap Is NOT Cute

It makes absolutely no sense that so many business owners are plagued with stagnation because they refuse to invest back into their business. They do nothing to grow their business because they believe that they need to be frugal about spending money. Here's a newsflash … you're not being frugal, you're refusing to successfully grow your business. You can't hold your purse straps tight and expect to grow a strong business. That's why I wrote my article, *You are not being savvy, you are being cheap* to help people understand that it takes money to make money:

It saddens me that some entrepreneurs would rather

31

allow their business to fold than to spend any money. These entrepreneurs experience all kind of woes because of their inability to spend money. You won't believe how many entrepreneurs tell me that they are not in a financial position to spend on their business but their hair is done, their nails look good and they are always talking about this event or party or going shopping.

Others have told me that they have wastefully spent money on unproductive results because they failed to vet the person promising them the world. I despise hearing the sob story of no money because I trusted the wrong. Guess what your bad! Try that story with your creditors and watch your credit score decline. So stop using people without vetting them first because at the end of the day it's your fault!

Now that I have that rant out of the way, let me offer you some ways to help you loosen the choke hold you have on your wallet and wisely spend money to grow your small business:

Always create options for your business. Limiting your options whether they are for contract work, products, or employees, will have you spending more money than you should. If a contractor promises you the world, then verify it. Check their references, ask other business owners in your circle and definitely Google them. I gave a contractor money for some paperwork, had to chase them down to get updates that I never got just to have my client tell me that the contractor never did the work. So I lost money and my client's trust. TIP: Always have at least three viable options, verify everything and then make an informed decision.

Update business needs before it matters. You should never place yourself in a position to be ill-equipped to perform the necessary tasks. If your computer is moving slow or crashing a lot, then upgrade the hard drive or buy another one. If you have dropped your smartphone so much that it acts dumb, then have the money ready to buy another one. TIP: Frequently check your inventory and buy in bulk instead of letting items run out. Don't wait until the need is there to find a solution.

Change how you view your expenses. Not all expenses are created equally. Some expenses are necessary and some can be excluded if you take the time to understand how each expense realistically and strategically fit into the mission for your business. TIP: Review your expenses and eliminate those expenses that are unproductive and costly.

When you take the approach to be cheap, you often agree to sacrifice quality. You can't afford anything new or even to network or advertise your business because you look at the associated costs all the time. You may even try to haggle people down on their prices. Shame on you either you pay the cost or move around. I get this often with the services The BLI Group offers. People want to haggle us about our costs for design, writing, production, apparel, PR, etc. We send out proposals only for people to pretend they can't afford the service they requested. They ask us for discounts, even if they are just a prospect. Eventually we got wise to these 'frugal' business owners approach to get something for nothing and we stopped budging on our price. You have to have the 'either pay or leave us the hell alone' mentality to protect your business.

You can't go to a large corporation and get free services or haggle them to pennies on the dollar. If you can, then great for you but I assure you, you will have a reputation of not being someone others should work with in no time. Unfortunately, it's a daunting task to change the mindset of someone who doesn't truly understand business and who particularly fails to understand the true value of their business and others.

It takes money to grow your business. Money to use other businesses for services; money to attract customers; money to grow. And if you think you can get the hookup on everything for your business, then you are the epitome of a con artist. Otherwise, you need to stop expecting people to understand your plight as an entrepreneur because the people you deal with are also entrepreneurs, so why hustle people you very well may need in the near future?

I use to get lassoed into the different plight stories. The 'I don't have money to pay you' or 'I don't have money because I am trying to build my company and my expenses are so large.' I failed to realize that I had expenses too and that my sons couldn't eat free services. Eventually, I got to the point where I only volunteer my services for my church, The Inspiring Body of Christ Church (IBOC) as a camera crew member. It took me getting sick and tired of being used and to understand that when you are in business everyone wants a handout.

So I know you get frustrated at folks constant needs. Just remember to tell yourself, 'My business is more important than an free opportunity.' It's okay to think about the growth of your business first, especially if someone wants to get a hook up or hand out. You have to remember that your business can't survive if you always have to be there for everyone else. I learned that from working for several publications for little to no money. They got quality articles and all I received was ended relationships when I asked for money or advertising in lieu of payment. Lesson learned.

And for the love of God, don't be the person who wastes other business owners' time when you know that you don't have the money to do business. I know you need to know the cost for their services or products, just ask. Make and decision and tell them if you are going to move forward. Don't make them wait for a response from you, if you know that you can't afford to buy from them. You wouldn't want anyone to do that to your business, so why do it to others? Their time, just like yours, is valuable and if you don't like your time being wasted, then think about that before you do unnecessary price inquiries about their services.

Going back to some of our previous clients who asked us

for a particular service. They came to us knowing that they didn't have the money but they proceeded to sign contracts, sometimes high dollar contracts and when it came time to pay the piper, we received nothing while they received finished work. What we did wrong was look at the portfolio building aspect of things instead of the obvious, that they were broke as a joke. We wasted countless hours and money chasing their dreams because we allowed their sob stories, their wishful thinking and their lies to get to our better judgment.

Save Money NOW!

As you know there are many drawbacks to owning your own business. And one of the drawbacks is saving money while trying to earn money. Everyone is trying to find feasible solutions for maintaining their business. Some struggle daily to open their doors, while others struggle to maintain their revenue stream. You have to be crafty when it comes to establishing a financial plan and budget for your business. You have to know every expense, accounts payable and receivables, and every source of income that your business brings in. I recommend talking to a CPA for ways to save money to grow your business. If you can't afford to meet with a CPA, then purchase an accounting software and track your finances that way.

You should have multiple streams of income but if you can't do that at the present time, then you need to cut unnecessary costs from your budget. If you don't need two cell phones and an office phone, then eliminate one or more of them. Google has toll free numbers for business owners who don't want to pay for landline services. This free service goes directly to your cell phone or landline. You can Skype to save money as well. Or Yahoo! Chat. Either method allows reduces your current phone charges. Oovoo is also an excellent choice for video chatting.

Save money on gas by picking a central location, if you don't have an office, to meet with clients or perspective clients. If you are meeting with perspective clients, then eliminate travel expenses by having a phone conference first. If they have to meet you in person, then take the necessary paperwork, such as contracts and invoices, with you so you can get them to sign before you leave. Always make sure every trip you take is worth it. If you have to deliver items to your clients, then be sure to charge a delivery fee. Gas is too high to drive around accommodating customers.

Consider consolidating your locations, if you have more than one and if you can. Having a storefront location is great but it can be costly with insurance premiums, utilities and other expenses. So if you have multiple locations or if you don't really need the location, then terminate your lease, if possible, so you can relocate to a more affordable area. Also, consider creating a home office in your living room or spare space. You can even consider office sharing with someone your trust. Just be sure to negotiate the terms for your benefit.

Save money on unnecessary collections and late fees by paying your debt on time. High interest rates and fees associated with poor debt management can literally eat all of your finances. To avoid losing money, pay your debt on time or make arrangements with your creditors to avoid unnecessary fees. I'll talk about how bad debt can impact your credit which directly affects the ability of your business to grow.

Where is My MONEY?!

Getting money owed to you from some clients can be a daunting task or it's just not going to happen. Eventually you're left with two choices, sue or let it go. Hopefully you don't have to do either but you do need to get your money. As a PR strategist and professional writer, I use to struggle to get monies owed to me from clients. I think the biggest insult is when I have to explain an invoice to a client repeatedly. It gets old fast. I had a client who requested various services and signed several contracts with me and when it came time to pay for the services she received, I had to explain her invoice and what services we completed repeatedly. Each time I explained it to her, it seemed that it would take that much longer to receive a payment. She even played the payment lost in the mail game. What a horrible trick to play on someone who requested and received services but refused to pay. If you have a similar situation to mine, then keep all email, phone and text correspondences just in case you have to sue or file a case against them with your local Better Business Bureau office.

That experience coupled with the so called self proclaimed natural hair diva who robbed us blind (to the tune of $9,500), I learned how to protect the interests of The BLI Group first. You have to realize that not receiving your money jeopardizes the growth of your business and damages the relationship between you and your client. That's undeniable. I have written countless articles on how to ensure accurate billing and getting paid on time. I have had to be my own case study too many times, so here are some tips I now use to get my money:

Invoice your clients on a set date to avoid delayed payments. Use QuickBooks and Microsoft Money to help you set invoice reminders or you can maintain a traditional invoicing system, such as Word or Excel. You just need to pick a date and send invoices to clients no more than 30 days out from the due date. I usually put my client's payment due date in their contract and advise them that even if they don't receive an invoice they are still responsible for paying their bill on time. I also assess a percentage based late fee every 30 days until the balance is paid.

Stick to a payment schedule. If you allow your clients to pay you whenever… STOP IT! Get on a payment schedule and stick to it. You can set any grace period you want. If you offer services, then get a retainer. We usually require a retainer ranging between 25-50 percent, depending on the contract amount. After that set your payment schedule to collect the remainder of the balance. Just don't release any project related items until all monies have been paid.

Add and collect all of the necessary fees owed to you. If your clients are always late, then you have to apply the necessary late, collection and legal fees, if applicable. Stop sweeping unpaid balances under the rug and taking financial losses. Meet with a bookkeeper, an accountant or just use some accounting software to figure out what's owed to you and then get to collecting.

Get a debt collector involved who will call past due clients. If you can't afford a debt collection agency, then make a deal with a debt collector for a nominal fee on each collected debt. This way you will receive part of your money and they will as well. Contact the Better Business Bureau to report clients who refuse to pay. Also, before you start any debt collection efforts, you must know your state laws on collecting debt from an individual. You don't want to get a case for harassment trying to get your money.

Barter for payments if and only if your client has a service that you can use but may not have the money to afford. If you want to go this route, then make sure you stay within the parameters of what's owed to you. You don't want to have the issue that I had when I allowed a client to work off her debt. Would you believe that I ended up owing her for services and I still don't know what she did. So my cautionary tale to you is to draw up a barter agreement that details the payment owed to you and the services that will be rendered to pay off the debt. Again, do not enter into a barter agreement unless you can use their services or product.

Your business won't survive if you are always willing to forgive the debt owed to you by your clients. Everyone and their mama has a sob story about their financial situations. So what?! Just remember that you will have the same issues if they don't pay you. It's time that you get your money on time, every time. Here is more detail on getting your money from my article *How to receive timely payments* (2010):

Do not negotiate or price haggle with your clients. Unless you are having a sale or a promotion you should not lower your prices to accommodate someone who states they are unable to use your services because of price. Clients are just as savvy with searching for a good deal and if they know you are willing to negotiate they will delay making payments. We have all sought to get a contract so much so that we were willing to work for pennies on the pennies that were never worth collecting. Don't do this. Set your prices and stick with them. Eventually the right clients will come who can afford your services and if you are a rock star entrepreneur, then those people will come faster than you think and will be more diverse.

Request a retainer. A retainer is usually a percentage of the final payment paid at the beginning of the contract to guarantee your services but for simple purposes a retainer is used to ward off clients who are not serious about patronizing your small business. Telling a client you charge an initial fee or percentage helps you with determining their ability to pay. You can even ask for half of the balance upfront or all of it depending on the amount. For my business, The BLI Group, we require full payments for orders under $1,000 upfront, especially on apparel and print orders. Yes we do get kick back but we know our worth and we won't budge to accommodate nonpayers or people looking for something for nothing.

Draw up a legal contract. The best contract should be drawn up by a lawyer and if you can't afford one then consult a legal specialist. Other than that use a contract specific to your industry and read it to verify it makes sense to you. Contracts should include payment, deliverables and a schedule for both parties to adhere to. Another good item to add to a contract is penalties for defaulting on the contract. Remember, you should always protect yourself first (which means your business) and then the client.

Include delinquent payment notices and details. Every invoice you send should include a delinquency notice. Many customers are afraid to become delinquent on their bills and do not want the hassle of collection calls; therefore, include a notice regarding collection processes for good measure. You own and operate a business so you have to stop thinking of everyone else before you think of your own survival. If you don't want to do that, then close up shop or turn your business into a nonprofit. Other than that charge people what they owe you and keep it moving.

Stop giving away free services. When you are looking for clients don't you tend to give services away for free? Yep. I know you do because even today I am still willing to throw in a free service to sweeten the deal but it's in a limited capacity. You have to set limits on free services and push for contracts or profitable means for payments. No exceptions. Either turn them into a customer or a charity case but your goal should always be for a customer who is willing to do repeat business and refer others.

Small businesses are just that, businesses and should be ran with the understanding that money is needed to grow, sustain and thrive. You cannot be successful by always thinking about your client's best interest because oftentimes they are not thinking about yours. If they were, then you would receive timely payments.

Pay Up or Serve Time

Regardless of your profitability or lack thereof, you still need to report your earnings and pay your taxes. Cutting corners is not wise by any stretch of the imagination when it comes to the Internal Revenue Services (IRS). Get with a tax professional or call the IRS to make sure you are right with your tax requirements and filing status. Failure to do so could result in fines, fees and penalties, up and including jail time. Don't believe me anyone who owes the IRS and they will tell you to pay your taxes.

You should be able to answer these questions without a shadow of a doubt:
1. Do you have an Employer Identification Number (EIN) or Taxpayer Identification Number (TIN)?
2. Are you claiming all of your deductions?
3. Are you reporting your business losses?
4. Are you reporting your revenue?
5. Are you maximizing your contributions?

If you have employees, then you need an EIN to report your earnings and to pay unemployment. You must also have W-2 (Wage and Tax Statement), W-3 (transmittal of Wage and tax Statement) or an I-9 form for them to complete. You need to know what's tax deductible and what's not; how to file a claim for those items or monetary contributions; and if you will receive any tax breaks for charitable contributions. These are just the basics when it comes to paying Uncle Sam his due. You should really consult a professional tax preparer or CPA who can make sure you are financially on track.

Business Credit is YOUR Credit

When I first started my business I received all types of

offers from creditors and suppliers who were willing to extend credit to me for my business. I learned quickly that despite their willingness to extend credit to me, I wasn't creditworthy. I had a lot of negative debt on my personal credit history which impeded my ability to get business credit. I didn't realize that my personal credit directly impacted my business credit. Just an FYI, when you apply for a Tax Identification Number (TIN), it is often times linked with your social security number (SSN), especially after other personal information is gathered about you.

Your TIN is not a new identity, it's still tied to you. That's why it is important to know where your credit score stands. If you have discrepancies on your credit, then contact the three major credit reporting agencies - Equifax, Transunion and Experian. For a fee, if you've already used the free report given yearly, they will send you a credit history report. Thoroughly go through the report to find any discrepancies such as resolved or incorrect debt that may be showing on your credit report. If you find any issues, then start the dispute process, which takes about 30 or so days to resolve.

Another way to keep up with your creditworthiness is through Duns and Bradstreet or D&B which offers businesses the opportunity to build business credit. A D-U-N-S Number, allows your business to apply for contractor jobs with corporations, the government and other entities. According to their website,

Most businesses underestimate how much current customers contribute to bad debt. The fact is, approximately 80 percent of bad debt is generated from accounts with a business relationship of longer than 12 months.

Why should so much bad debt be generated by old

customers, especially after you've done careful screening? The reason is that because of the increasingly dynamic nature of business, your initial business credit check cannot be expected to predict financial risks far into the future.

As an example, for every 1,000 customers, you can expect 200 will report significant changes each year that potentially could impact their business credit.

To keep up with rapid changes, you must monitor these regularly to ensure your business is safe. A key will be getting current business credit reports on existing customers to improve your ongoing business evaluation (DNB.com, 2013).

You don't want to be in a position where you need something for your business but can't get it because of your credit. Take time to stay abreast of your credit history and score. Remember that your TIN is not a free pass, it is designed to see how much you're earning a year. Always make smart choices with your personal credit because it affects your business credit. And that's how you financially commit to your business.

Get Your Money on Your Mind Right

For this chapter, I want you to look at your finances and really determine if you can sustain a business or is it really just a hobby you overindulge:

1. How much money or percentage do I reinvest in my business?
2. What money management tools am I using?
3. Do I consistently invoice my clients? Why or why not?
4. How often am I asked for a discount and how often do I oblige?
5. What ways am I financially hurting my business?
6. Does my company have incentive programs for my employees or clients?
7. What are my policies for returns, discount requests or other financial breaks?
8. How am I maximizing my company's growth? List at least 5 ways.

Chapter Three

Alignment

How many times have you fussed about something being too hard? Or that you had to operate your business alone? I'm the first person to raise my hand because I have absolutely no qualms about being honest that owning a business is hard work. I use to do it all and it wore me out and down. So my advice to you, don't try to wear all of the different hats that it takes to run a business. You seriously need to consider having an accountant, a legal advisor, a HR consultant, a mentor and other key people to help your grow and even sustain your business. No, you can't do it alone. I don't care what you say.

One of my clients, Lasonda Campbell, the author of *Passion Power Play* and a serial entrepreneur wrote a great go-to guide for entrepreneurs. In the chapter, The Player's Union, Campbell talks about having a winning team. Her advice is to align yourself with other like-minded people who understand your passion. You can't be successful doing everything alone. Campbell provides you with a way to find and align yourself with the right people in her book and I want to tell you what I think about having the right team.

You need to be aligned with the right people. SIMPLE. So stop looking for someone to carry you or sponsor your next big idea because you will either look like a pushover or a user. What you need to have is a powerful team of people who truly want to go where you are going and who have the means, rather financial, educationally or just the plain old drive to get you there. In searching for the right people to help me grow my business, I wrote a three part article series called W*ho Do You Have an Alliance With?* in 2010. These articles were inspired by the teachings of Pastor Rush and they will help you understand who should be on your team:

We all know that in business we are told to form alliances with like-minded people and similar businesses who can further our agenda for a more stable and productive company but no one tells us who to and how to strategically form alliances. The right alliance will allow us to prosper whereas the wrong alliance will drain us financially, mentally, man-power and other detrimental business affairs. We have to be steadfast in forming the right alliances to always guarantee the growth of our companies.

We have to be wise about our alliances that they do not detract from our spiritual connection with our heavenly father, God and Jesus. Far too many times we are more focused on the bottom line of our business rather than the bottom line of spiritual walk with Jesus Christ and we become distracted in what we are called to do, which is build the kingdom of God. Now I am not saying speak in tongues, pour holy oil on every person you meet but I am saying you need to understand that your alliances can cause you to lose and not gain in business and in your spiritual walk.

Here are some tips for checking those around you:

If you start to speak negatively and those around you always agree with you then you are around the wrong person. The Bible says, so as a man speaks he is. When you are around people who always agree with your negativity, even if it is brief, and never tries to encourage you in the word then you are around the wrong individual or group of people. These people can be business associates, partners, or employees.

Do the people you do business with keep you in the past? Sometimes, like Lot's wife we focus on what we left behind and fail to see what is in front of us. It becomes hard to look at the future when you are continuously encouraged to look behind you. The alliances you form should always encourage you to move ahead and understand the blessings you currently have and that are coming, the seen and unseen.

Your alliance with people in business should always be a healthy one. Of course you are going to get into some incidents with people but because of the God in you, you should never burn any bridges unless you are instructed by the Spirit of God to do so. (But that is another topic all together). Who are you around that are hindering you from fully prospering in the blessing called your business?

Do you have 'Yes Men' or God's men, or women, around you? People who know you are blessed often attach themselves to you because they may not believe in their own blessings but they surely know you are favored, or fortunate as they may have claimed. A person who is willing to tell you yes all the time is not the person you want around you all the time. When Jesus was spreading the good news of God he his own disciples doubted, questioned and did not believe in Him totally but they followed Him around and Peter in particular spoke his mind when was in opposition of Jesus' direction. Now if Jesus can have people around Him with their own opinions why can't you?

Do the people you do business with allow you to talk about God or do they shut you down? You know you have an unholy alliance when you attempt to talk about God and Jesus and they tell you they do not want to hear it or they become busy. While you are to still speak of God you should not alliance yourself with someone who does not believe in the same God you believe in. No I do not have to be political correct when I say that if one of your business constituents do not believe in God then you should not do business with them. Guess what? Discourse for God is contagious. In Isaiah 31:1 it says to be careful of people not seeking God.

People expectations of you and your business are high when you step forward and proclaim your love and mission for God. You will experience attacks from every different direction because Satan now has a reason to single you out and pick on you, so to speak, to see if he can get you to change sides. He will even go as far as to place people in your business circle who will form an alliance with you and turn your world upside down. You have to understand who you are forming an alliance with.

Here are some additional tips:

Never commit yourself to someone you know is not willing to go the distance with you. Business is a grueling attack on the senses sometimes and oftentimes you pick up business partners and employees who you know are only around for a short time. They never fully contribute to where you are going but because of their personality or ability to be there, whatever that means, you keep them around.

Have new business opportunities just appeared? Yes Satan wants to take you out and he is cunning enough to send you some wonderful business opportunities. You think you have it made and have made the right decision to go in with someone who possesses the right qualities, i.e. they talk about God but never really show their commitment to him, and then the next thing you realize you are at a loss in profits, morale and even employees. Satan is so cunning Peter warns us of his desires for our lives in I Peter 5:8 – *Be sober, be vigilant; because your adversary the devil walks about like a roaring lion, seeking whom he may devou*r. Don't be on the menu.

Your customers, business partners, vendors, suppliers and employees are always looking at you to determine if you are who you really say you are in Christ. You have to be diligent when you pursue God that He guides you to the alliances which build the kingdom of God rather than destroy it. Do not allow the desire to grow your business to overshadow your need for developing your spirit.

Despite being written three years ago this article is still very relevant because it applies to anyone who wants to have a business relationship or even a partnership with others. You have to know who you are aligned with. It's relevant to the success of your business.

Knowing Your Business Partner

With the exception of my first business partner, Stephanie Washington, who had no choice but to pull back because I didn't understand the concept of getting paid for what we did; and my current business partner, Eric Bettis, I can't tell you how much time I've wasted trying to beg people to be my business partner. They said they wanted what I presented to them but when it was time to work, they disappeared faster than a Genie after three wishes. I've had at least five business partners since 1998. Sad really but I understood that I couldn't run a major company alone. God had given me a large vision and I needed help so I settled time and time again. If you have a partner or are considering a partner, then you need to create a partnership agreement that outlines the responsibilities, roles, duties, financial obligations and other important details for each partner. A handshake is not going to work these days.

Because I have a history of running through business partners like water running through the hand, I have identified, again from my experience, traits that people tend to have. Understanding these business partner personality types will help you avoid the bad business partners and find a good one:

The Dreamer. This person has more dreams, more ideas and more plans than Disney World. They are always thinking of a new something but never really perfecting any of their ideas. You will spend countless hours trying to help this person lasso one dream to accomplish. They are innovative, if guided.

The Doubter. This person doubts everything they see, even if they put it together. They have little to no patience with people or you and are always looking for the exit door. You will spend more time trying to get them on board and to be positive than you will get actual work done. They also complain a lot and eventually their complaining will rub off on or drain you. They require tangible results frequently.

The Busybody. I have been called this a time or two. The busybody is someone who has to be everywhere, doing everything and knowing everyone. They can't sit still long enough to finish a project. They come up with some of the best ideas but refuse to put forth the effort to pull them off the plan together to make it work. They oftentimes lack focus and typically like instant gratification. They are great task assigners because they always see the next big thing.

The Avoider. This person doesn't want to make decisions. They let their personal life interfere with business. They just avoid being responsible for any major business decisions. They prefer a limited role of responsibility. They will do the work but they definitely don't like to be the lead.

The Diva. The diva wants money for work that hasn't been completed. They want compliments and all the attention. If they don't get the attention they believe they deserve, then they cause problems by avoiding or doubting. They are hard to deal with because they have a 'it's all about me' personality.

The Eager Novice. The eager novice is hard to deal with because they often jump into situations without full knowledge of it. They tend to hold onto their ideas rather than using the ideas of others. They easily offend and become defensive. On the other hand, they have a lot of good ideas but yet in still those ideas require a lot of grooming to make sound decisions for the team and company.

There are many more business partner personality types but these are the ones I have encountered over the years. Dealing with one or more of these personality types has often caused me slow down for them to catch up. But the one thing I know is … who God calls, He qualifies. So if you have to constantly focus on your business partner or the people around you in business, then he/she may not be right for you. During one of my so-called business partner endeavors, I wrote *Finding a trustworthy business partner* (2011). It was written to help readers understand the qualities needed in a business partner:

Some key characteristics to consider when looking for that right person to assist you with your business venture are:

1. They possess integrity. Business partners should operate with integrity at all times. The integrity of a person will determine if you are able to leave important matters in

their care and they will be accomplished without mistakes or falsification.

2. They are ethical. Being ethical in business is a personal characteristic that is often lost in the desires to succeed. Entrepreneurs may resort to some unsavory tactics to get the job done. If you are not a person with unethical characteristics neither should your business partner should not be either. You want to sustain the trust of your clients not lose it.

3. They are straightforward. This characteristic can be tricky and misconstrued with rude. The last type of person you need on as your business partner is "Yes Man". A "Yes Man" is a person that agrees with every idea you have even if it is bad. You need someone who when asked or not asked gives their honest and respectable opinion on what should or should not be done for the benefit of the business. A person that is rude does not care about their delivery and if often pushy with their ideals.

4. They are honest. Honesty is the best policy is the old adage regarding how to deal with people. Your business partner should be honest with you and honest with your clients. A dishonest business person only sees the bottom line of making cash and does not often think of their actions past the transactions. You want someone you can trust to be honest with you and you clients.

5. They are trustworthy. Not trusting your business partner is the first sign that you do not have the right partner. You have to trust your business partner and your employees to take you to the next level of success.

Barbara Corcoran from Shark Tank was a guest speaker at the 2013 *Entrepreneur Magazine's* Growth Conference in Dallas and she told the audience, "You need to be with people who are going where you are going. If you are an outgoing person, then you need an organizer... that person who will keep things running. You need the ying and yang balance in your business relationships to be truly successful."

As you look for the right business relationship or partner, be sure that their character align with yours. They don't have to be identical to you but they should have the same desires for success that you have. You shouldn't have to beg, slow down, or stop to keep them happy and around. Be sure to listen to your gut and get feedback from those closest to you before signing any agreements. Your partner should increase business not deter it.

Employees – You're Hired???

If you're fortunate to have someone work for you, then you are definitely growing your business. Unfortunately, most businesses experience turnover because they hire the wrong people. Even large companies experience this pitfall but they can recover because they have the budget to cycle through employees. You, on the other hand, need to pick the right people from the start because when you lose an employee, you become the employee.

I have had several conversations with great friend Tamara Starks, serial entrepreneur, new mom and wife, and in one of her many businesses where she has employees she mentioned the challenges she has with employees who aren't right for her clientele. So with that I decided to go back into the archives to pull out excerpts my article entitled *The right people for your small business*, which is a part of my series called *The 5Ps of small business ownership*:

> The people you have working for your small business may very well be the determining factor in your success or failure. When selecting employees, whether part- or full-time, it is important to know the following:
> Let your employees know the expectations in the beginning. When you are seeking to hire new employees they should understand the vision and mission of your small business. Without a clear vision or mission of the company many employees become wayward and attempt to operate independently of the company rules and guidelines. Establish order from the beginning to ensure compliance in the end.
> Add interest to your employee's job. Your employees

are not robot capable of performing the same mundane tasks day in and day out; therefore, it is important for you to add variety to their workday to show you are interested in maintaining their employment and offering them a fun work environment. No you do not need to have a party everyday but adding value like a small commission for selling products or contests will give your employees something to shoot for at work.

Include your employees in your promotional efforts. Your employees may offer you some of the best and sound information you have ever received therefore it is wise to inquire their feedback regarding promotions. Use your meeting times as information gathering sessions to assist you with attracting new clients and keeping current ones.

It has often been said that you are only as successful as your best employee. You can't live in a glass bubble thinking that people should just be happy with a job because times are hard. If you take that approach I guarantee you, you will not stand a chance at having a business without constant turnover. Your employees can literally make or break your business, so hire the right ones from the start and like Corcoran said, "Let them go if they are not being productive earlier than later." This is even true for family and friends.

Another one of my clients, who owns a high-end spa, has a problem with finding the right employees. Not because she is a horrible boss but because she failed to implement policies, procedures and a commitment to them. When I visited her spa I noticed how they disregarded her until she raised her voice. They were literally taking her kindness for weakness. I can't stand to see employees take advantage of their employers. And on the same end of things, I can't stand to see employers take advantage of their employees. So where am I going with this? To an article I wrote called *How to save your business from pandemonium*:

If you are finding yourself in a position where you are unable to effectively lasso good employees and everything is falling on your shoulders, then you maybe in the midst of a business meltdown. You need to take immediate action to restructure your business and get your employees on the right track before you lose clients and your good employees. The restructure phase can be a lengthy one if immediate actions are not taken to resolve internal issues with your employees.

Take control NOW by:

Calling a staff meeting. Issues can be addressed in a formal staff meeting. In a staff meeting employees are able to address their concerns while you act as the mediator for any hostilities or concerns your staff may have. Staff meetings will also allow you to set goals for the day, week or month. You need to have staff meetings frequently and be consistent with them. Your employees will only respond how you respond and if you have a hostile or nonchalant approach to handling business so will they. So make sure your staff meetings have an agenda and purpose where your employees, and you, can have realistic takeaways to grow the business and foster healthy relationships.

Plan employee developmental programs. Having an ill-prepared staff is one of the issues which can lead to discourse within your company. If your company deals with certain specialties services, then you should make sure your staff is current on training and certifications. Individual staff development programs are beneficial to increase and uplift your staff. Employee development programs do not have to be expensive, especially if you are current with your industry knowledge. You can take a weekend to teach your employees new industry requirements or find free resources online.

Make time for your employees and business. Your employees may require some one-on-one time and therefore you should make yourself available at least once a week for the time they need. This one-on-one time with your employees is helpful to learn about what they are doing, where they want to go and how you can assist them. If you don't know your employees then you put yourself in a position to be robbed by them. Not saying that employees are like that but let's be real. You need to update their files and check on them. The spa client I just mentioned didn't know that her employees were stealing from her and offering free services to their family and friends. She literally lost hundreds of thousands of dollars having a hands off approach with her employees. You can't do that, regardless how big your business is. You have to make time or hire a manager to help you.

Terminate employees and contractors who are not productive. Pandemonium can be caused from unproductive employees and others who work closely with your business. Their inability or desire to perform the necessary tasks to take your business to the next level should be terminated immediately. The publication I worked for experienced pandemonium because of the employees who just didn't want to work. Advertisers were constantly talking to someone different and that made the company look unstable. So avoid this pitfall early by getting rid of the trash. If you need sales people and they don't perform within 60 days get rid of them. If you hire a management or PR services firm and you don't get a new opportunity within the first 30 days get rid of them. If you have a designer who takes more than two weeks to render you a first version design 86 then immediately. Stop wasting your time waiting on people to do what you hired them to do. No exceptions!

Be proactive rather than reactive when determining the best solutions for your business. Pandemonium will stifle and ruin your business if issues are not addressed immediately. Your business deserves to grow and be productive.

You would be surprised how business owners still don't take the time to do what they have to do when it comes to getting rid of people who mean nothing to the growth of their business. You can misalign yourself with the wrong employees, business partners, or constituents. It maybe because you have a heart of gold and want to help everyone you meet. But like the Bible says, and I am paraphrasing, being unevenly yoked is a detriment to the believer. Again, I am paraphrasing but this simply means don't waste your time being aligned with the wrong people in business or your personal life for that matter.

Get Your Mind and Inner Circle Right

Now I am going to challenge you to look around you to determine who you have in your inner circle for your business. Ask yourself these questions and if the folks you have identified don't align with your answers, then cut them loose or reduce their necessity in your company.

1. Does he/she really assist me when I need him/her?
2. Do I have to ask more than a couple of times for things to get done?
3. Is there always some kind of drama going on in their personal life that takes away from business?
4. Has my business grown since aligning with them?
5. How many customer complaints have we had since they became a part of the team?
6. Are they making the necessary sacrifices to grow my business?
7. Do I honestly have to make most of the decisions alone although this is a partnership?
8. Will the business really suffer if I cut them loose?

Chapter Four

Clients

I often have to take a deep breath when it comes to thinking about and having clients. Some of my clients are wonderful while others are just flat out terrible. Yes, I said terrible but if you know anything about having a business, then you know you have your good and bad clients. Eventually, you learn to deal with different types of clients, the good, the bad, and the ugly ones. All of these clients help you foster a respect for dealing with people and ultimately help you grow your business.

The one thing I want you to always remember is… you pick your clients. Ding. Zinga. Whatever sound you need me to make so you understand that you pick the people who will either support you or destroy you. It's called picking your own Judas. Just like Jesus did, we have a tendency to pick the people who will cause us pure hell. Why? Maybe we like drama; or maybe we think we can mold them; maybe we honestly just don't know why we have them around but we always seem to have someone around us who will cause some level of trouble in our professional lives and honestly that can keep us grounded.

Just take a moment to clear your mind. Now ask yourself, 'Do I believe that all money is good money?' If you do, then you are headed down the wrong path. Clients who have ulterior motives look for business owners who will jump at a dollar.

When you focus on money you can't discern which clients are beneficial to you and which ones will make you want to catch a case. Far too often we take for granted that God has given us the spirit of discernment and understanding. We fail to see the actual situation at hand because of our own selfish agenda. And what happens when the will of God is removed from our decision making? Chaos. We give the devil free will to destroy the vision that God gives us and that's when our businesses suffer.

How many times have you thought to yourself, *'I really don't need to take on a new client.' 'I really need to get rid of this client.' 'I need to end a toxic relationship with a client.'?* How often do you pray to God for bless something you know He never qualified or wanted you to get involved in? Don't count because you won't be able to finish reading my book. Being involved with the wrong clients is detrimental not only to your business but to your reputation. It can keep you from executing the vision that God gave you. You have to be mindful of the gifts that God gave you.

"Therefore you do not lack any spiritual gift as you eagerly wait for our Lord Jesus Christ to be revealed," 1 Corinthians 7.

This scripture lets you know that you have the gifts of God and the Holy Spirit and that it is important for you to use your gifts according to the will of God. Whenever you have the opportunity to bring on a new client, then you also need to earnestly pray about that client. Just like you need to pray about your other connections. Don't be afraid to trust your instincts. If you get a bad feeling, then hold off on servicing that client. Product based companies are different but for a service based company, be mindful of the clients you take on.

You can avoid the frustration of dealing with clients who maybe on assignment from Satan to block your blessings and destroy your business. Yes, Satan assigns people to you to create chaos in your life. Your charge is to be steadfast and know within yourself what's of God and what's not. Just like every business opportunity, you must pray about every client.

Don't get caught up in the mega money that can be made, the exposure you can receive for your business, or the clients that will overflow. Don't do it. I promise you, you will regret it. I have had countless encounters where a client promised me this or that if I worked with them for a discount, hookup or for free, only to fight with them when it was time to make good on their end. The nerve. But these are the situations where I didn't seek God and if I did, I didn't wait for His response.

Committing To Your Clients

Committing to your clients don't mean trying to become their friend. I have had to learn that lesson the hard way. I use to involve my clients, a select few, in my personal business, bad business relationships and everything in between. It was apparent that after my life turned upside down and my clients started to jump ship that we were not friends. They paid me for a service and that's what they expected to receive. I no longer attempt to befriend my clients. I'm not saying you can't become friends over time but your clients are just that … your clients.

I know that I have been harping on commitment but it's important for you to commit your mind, time, money and energy to growing your business. In my article, *Managing your commitment to your clients (2011)* I talked about the following ways to commit to the good clients:

Commit to getting to know your clients. As an entrepreneur it is easy to get to know your customers until you are balancing more clients than you know what to do with. Therefore, you should periodically collect pertinent information such as special days, email addresses and the like to send out special greetings during the holidays and special occasions. Nothing beats a handwritten note or thank you card that is not electronic. Cass Butler, owner of The Butler Enterprise specializes in still sending her clients a handwritten thank you note. The return for being personal and remembering the small things is a connection with your clients and a continued relationship.

Commit to following up with your clients. Following up with your clients is essential to establishing repeat business or receiving additional inquiries from new clients. You never want to leave the impression that you are unresponsive when it comes to inquiries or just general feedback. Your clients either talk about how effective you are or how ineffectively you handle your business communications. If you can spend hours on social liking statuses and re-tweeting, then surely you can take time to send a follow-up email or better yet pick up the phone and talk to them personally. Geesh, don't over technology yourself out of a client.

Commit to offering your clients more. Giving a discount here and there is not the value added benefit your clients expect. With major corporations are offering clients discounted and free services; rapid response and customer service; and a plethora of other services, you have to be able to offer your clients perks. Consider a reward system where clients can earn free services or products once a certain number is reached; have a giveaway of sorts for your clients; the possibilities are endless.

If you are good to your clients they will be good to you. You can increase your commitment to your customers by getting to know your clients general information; following up with your clients; and offering your clients more than just a discount. Your clients will respect your loyalty to them in the long run.

But then there are those cases where bad clients, who pretend to be good clients, suck the life out of you. Not literally, but it sure can seem like it. I have had my fill of the worst of worst clients. Especially those who pretend to want a personal relationship with me just to get tips and services for free. We have all been there where a client attaches themselves to you and pretend they like you all the while sucking your brain dry of information. Well it's time to unhook that leech so you can focus on your good clients.

Bad Clients Be Gone

It is an undeniable fact that as you strive for excellence in your business there will always be someone to insult you, tarnish your reputation or downright be difficult to work with no matter how hard you try to help them. Sometimes it's enough to make you wonder if you're doing the right thing with having a business, especially if you just started. You may have lost sleep or your appetite trying to figure out what you did wrong or where did you find a client that grieves you so much.

Fortunately, there are remedies for getting non-beneficial clients off of your client list so you can continue to chart the best course of action for success. You need to focus on maintaining your good clients and finding more like them. When you come to a point where you feel like you want to give up because of the never satisfied client, don't. Just start the process of getting rid of difficult clients. Start with your business plan to determine who your target audience is. If you didn't identify your target audience in your business plan, then you need to identify one immediately.

You can also review your current client list to determine which clients you consider to be good, bad or ugly. Your goal when reviewing your client list is to eliminate the ugly clients first, then work to get rid of the bad clients. Ideally, you want all good clients but let's be real, it won't happen. So get rid of the ones who are hurting your business first. These are the clients who constantly complain, never or rarely pay on time, and cause delay in some way. Let these people go.

You can draw in the wrong clients based on the products or services you offer. Yes, it's possible to attract the wrong client just by being in business. These are the people that shop for deals and if you offer what they want, they will find you. So in order to avoid deal seekers who will not become loyal clients, take the time to review your products or services and only keep those items that attract your target audience. To add to that, stop offering what they want. Yes, it's that simple and it's not discrimination. It's only discrimination when you tell anyone that they're the reason you decided to eliminate something. That's called a lawsuit, so keep your mouth closed and make the necessary changes to your products/services to get rid of clients who are not in your target audience.

Policies and procedures are needed for operating your business. You won't be successful if you're creating and implementing policies and procedures based on bad client experiences. Establishing firm policies and procedures from the start, will let your clients know exactly what to expect and when. Remember when Wal-Mart took back anything without a receipt to verify if they sold it? If not, then you know why they changed that policy fast, because people were bringing back items that other stores sold and Wal-Mart was losing money. I've seen last minute policies and procedures created for payments, fees and services to be rendered after bad experiences. The problem with waiting to implement these policies and procedures, is that your clients get used to doing what they want, when they want. You need a foundation built first so you can save yourself the headache of dealing with clients who aren't willing to follow your policies.

When you have the same consistent no good clients, you just maybe attracting who you are as a person and business owner. Did I really just say that? Yes, I did. What are your motives for being in business? Do you want to leave a legacy or make a quick buck? If it's the latter, you will understand Notorious B.I.G.'s famous words, "More money, more problems." Clients will pay you just to drive you crazy so don't get caught in the money trap by chasing dollars.

Don't let bad clients cause you to lose your passion for owning a business. It's important to know your worth. Define who you are and what your business is about from the beginning. Don't wait until things get misaligned to get a solid plan together for dealing with difficult clients. Get your mind right now to avoid trouble later.

Customer Base 101

By now you should have a good idea if you have what it takes to start a business. You really have to have the wherewithal to deal with the different aspects of business and to grow it. You have to make your business a necessity for your clients. You have to make sure they come to you first, and in some cases, only come to you. So do you know how to do that? There are ways outside of social media to increase your business' exposure. These opportunities can be cost effective if you take the proper measures to ensure the information you give about your business is relevant and customer focused.

You want to make every effort to stay in contact with your customers. Posting on Facebook and Twitter is not staying in contact with your customers, that's called entertainment. I know that there are businesses that are successful using social media but nothing beats traditional marketing. You can stay in contact with your customers by being creative. Create a newsletter, send out weekly, bi-weekly or monthly correspondence, just stay in contact with them the way that they prefer to be contacted. Kristi Jackson, MBA founder of Women CEO is always finding the latest and greatest communication tools for CEOs. She suggests that you use Constant Contact, MailChimp and other email campaign tools that allow you to stay in contact with your customers, current, and potential. You can import the address book from your primary email account and send templates or self-created emails to your customers. The abundant opportunities for using these applications will help you create and maintain customer loyalty.

Don't be known for being the king or queen of sales. Instead, Offer discounts when they matter. Don't offer discounts because you are in a financial pinch because you will regret it with the types of customers you attract. Consider offering discounts when they matter to your client. You will notice that your clients will be loyal to you when they feel that they have a deal no one else can get. Space your discounts and sales out so you can attract new clients and build customer loyalty.

If you want to know how you are doing, just ask your customers how you are doing. Doing this makes them feel as if their input is valuable to your business. Make a suggestions box, send emails, postcards, or ask them when the visit you but collect the data necessary to learn how you can increase customer loyalty. Just be prepared to hear all of the feedback they offer and use it to improve your business and the experience of your customers.

Another way to build customer loyalty is by showing your customers appreciation. Celebrity cake designer Porsha "Cake Diva" Kimble holds private cake tastings for her loyal clients to show her appreciation. Lara Michelle, owner of Legendary

Beauty Spa and Salon and her own makeup line, Lara Michelle, provides her loyal customers with free upgrade services. Celebrity makeup artist, Riska Crowder goes above and beyond to offer her loyal customer a free service after so many visits. I could go on and on but you get the point. You need to show your customers just how valuable they are to you.

In this day and age, where businesses come a dime a dozen, you have to take extra precautions to add value to your business. Send out greetings cards, host a customer appreciation event, just do something to add value for your customers. Trust me, new customers will want to become a part of your dedicated customer base because you show your current customers appreciation. Your business deserves abundance. So what are you going to do about creating it?

Get Your Mind Right For Your Clients

It's time to answer the questions about your clients and how they do and do not impact your growth. Remember a bad client can throw you off.

1. What has been the hardest client related issue that I have had to overcome? How did I handle it? What did I learn from it?
2. Have I honestly identified my target audience?
3. How many clients can I get rid of without hurting my business?
4. When I decided to market to my clients what am I really giving them that is of value?
5. Do I even know who my loyal clients are and what they want?
6. What tools am I using to grow my customer base or even to stay in contact with them?
7. Have I done research on the trends and staples in my industry that will be marketable to my clients?
8. What is my social media strategy and how am I using it to grow my business?

Chapter Five

Growth

$\mathbf{Y}$ou have to take every opportunity to stay current with the latest must haves and to dos. What you don't have to do is take part in the latest trends in your industry. There are times when you may feel overwhelmed with what you need to do to ensure the growth of your business. But keep cool. Get your head out of the clouds because this is business, not high school. You have to be strategic about what opportunities you need to take and which ones you need to avoid.

It's just that simple. Think of the company, large or small, that took advantage of every opportunity that was presented to them, they ran themselves into the ground literally. Or the company that failed to take advantage of certain opportunities, they disappeared. Can't think of one, Blockbuster is one that disappeared and Starbucks is one that took too many growth opportunities so they had to close down a lot of stores.

Don't be like these companies.

First, know that your company can't be successful if you aren't willing to be on the Internet. You need your own website. Not a Wordpress site, not a social media page … you need a website so people can find you. In case you didn't know, most people research your business before they ever do business with you. What impression are you leaving if people can't find you? Traditional word of mouth and ground work is important when growing your business but it's not the only investment you need to make to grow its presence and reach. A quality website is a sound investment to have. Move away from the cookie cutter web designs and towards a more professional look. Just ask around and do your research on the company, the cost and turnaround time.

Depending on your business, your current market may currently be saturated with more than enough businesses that offer similar products or services. So what do you do? Travel. In order to develop relationships and client bases in other markets, you have to be willing to move around. Traveling stylist, independent sales persons, etc. use this option when looking for new clients. So why don't you? Traveling to other markets positions your business for growth and that's what you want your business to do … grow!

You can't just jump at every opportunity that comes in front of you, so you have to be strategic. Nowadays you have to do more than just sell a product or service, you need to generate additional streams of revenue to grow your business. This may mean upselling additional products or services; launching a new service or product; or starting a subsidiary company under your parent company. Either way you should carefully consider all of your options before you add to the growth of your business.

Education is Key

In order for your business to be successful you have to remain knowledgeable of the trends in your industry. I didn't say you have to participate in every trend but you need to know what the heck is going on. It bothers me when business owners don't know what's going on but they call themselves an expert. How can you expect clients to support you if you don't know what's going on with your business? You have to stay current with market trends in your industry that will help you grow your business. Financial advisors do it, sales professionals do it, basically anyone worth their weight in gold make sure they stay abreast of market trends. So get on the ball and stop acting entitled or worse, being lazy.

One way to remain current within your industry is to educate yourself. I don't care what you say, you need to have some form of education, especially as a business owner. I wouldn't dare refer a anyone to a business owner who doesn't take the time to know their industry or their business. I worked hard to earn my degrees but I continue to stay abreast about my profession and industry. I read books and articles; I talk to industry leaders who are more experienced than I am; I do everything I can to know what I'm talking about when I meet with a client. So I except you to have the same dedication. Industry standards rarely remain the same, so do your business a huge favor and remain educated. My article, *The importance of educating yourself*, addresses the need to stay educated:

> I think one of my biggest pet peeves is when someone starts a business and refuses to be educated about particular industry. Just like a hair stylist has to understand the processes for styling and maintaining a client's hair or a doctor must learn medicine before they are able to treat a patient legally, business owners need to understand the importance of their particular industry or field.
>
> Many entrepreneurs understand that their business will increase in viability through education. Unfortunately, owning a business may have limited your full-time educational pursuits. Entrepreneurs can gain new industry knowledge through new and traditional education settings.
>
> Consider these various educational settings if education has been on your mind:
>
> Online Colleges. The online college environment is one which has increased in popularity over the past 10 years and shows no signs of slowing down. These colleges offer working adults the convenience through online access to obtain a degree, from associates to doctorate, in a vast

variety of educational fields. But there are drawbacks to obtaining a degree online, the high costs and acceptance of your degree. Consider your current small business demands and income before enrolling for an online college.

Traditional College. Traditional colleges are the foundation of the higher education system because of the solid foundation and personal interaction between students and instructors. Traditional colleges offer a variety of courses but can yield high expenses, a long commute and strenuous admission policies. Be sure to check your availability, out of pocket expense and alternatives before applying for admissions

Community College. Community colleges are typically centrally located with various campuses; limited individual courses and degreed programs; and low costs. Before enrolling be sure your small business needs can be met through attendance at a community college.

Trade Schools. Trade schools are one of the fastest option for education but also a tricky option because of issues with reputability and high costs for short learning periods. Trade schools offer technical skills such as medical billing and coding, cosmetics, auto repair and so on. Consider your trade school with great care.

Distance Learning. Typically distance learning programs offers courses and certification programs which is a plus for degreed or knowledgeable small business owners. Distance learning programs are often offered online and at a college campus. Also distance learning courses are affordable. If you need to take a brush-up course or obtain a certificate, distance learning may be your best option.

Not only is educating yourself important, it's also important to develop your talents daily. How do you do that? Just do it. It's not hard. If you're a writer, then write every day. If you're an educator, then learn so you can teach others. You get my drift? You have to constantly develop your talents in order to benefit your clients. My childhood friend and noted hairstylist in our hometown of Kansas City, KS, Latreena Lambert has been a licensed hairstylist since she was a teenager but she constantly educates herself about the hair and beauty industry. She practices her skills daily, goes online to see what other hairstylists are doing, attends seminars, conferences and workshops around the country, puts herself in front of industry leaders who can show her new techniques, designs and the like. She is constantly developing her talents because she is passionate about what she does and where she wants to go.

Another thing you need to do is educate yourself about what you can and can't do. You need to know the legalities of your industry such as what materials you can use that are public domain or under copyright/trademark. My best friend, Ebony Holmes, owner of Buttercream Belle in Baton Rouge, LA, a custom home bakery company, researched her behind off before she ever baked a cake for a customer. She knew what cakes she could and couldn't bake because of legal parameters. But she is surprised when she people making cakes just because someone is paying for it.

"It bothers me when my clients ask for a Disney cake or a high-end designer cake like Coach, because I can't design those cakes. It's illegal to reproduce images that belong to companies that are trademarked or copyrighted without their expressed consent," says Holmes. "That's why it's important for people to educate themselves on the dos and don'ts of business before they find themselves in trouble and not knowing is no excuse."

You need to develop your talents daily so you don't look crazy when you meet with a client. Write. Sing. Draw. Design. Teach. Talk. Whatever you have to do to develop yourself for your clients, most importantly for yourself, then do it. Stop waiting for knowledge to just drop out of the sky. Please stop being arrogant. Stop thinking you got this, you know what you're doing because I guarantee you that even the most experienced individual continues to learn and hone their talents. If you can't afford to do what Lambert and Holmes did to grow their businesses, then networking is your next best option.

Network, Not Hang Out

Few people truly understand the sacrifices of starting and maintaining a business. Yet in still, only a few people are willing to sacrifice to make their business grow. You have to be willing to work long hours, have sleepless nights and work for little to no money when you start a business. A quote that I have found to be true is, "the first 3-5 years your business owns you," author unknown. Think about that. If you think you can start a business so you can own something you are sadly mistaken. You own nothing but the title and if you're not good at running your business, then you don't own that either. But I digress.

Networking is an important tool that allows you to gather, meet and exchange contact information with other likeminded business people. The networking savvy entrepreneur travels for conferences, attend events, and workshops to stay abreast of opportunities to grow their business. Opportunity is what they seek and networking is how they find it. What are you doing?

Let me say this … start networking outside of your 'clique.' You know that group of people that you always see at the same events? Stop it because the chances of you getting work from them is slim to none. Even if you have the fortune of working together, don't limit yourself by always dealing with the same people who are also looking to grow their business. Branch out for Pete's sake. And don't rely on them for opportunities because they are looking for success just like you are.

Professional and nonprofit organizations sometimes host free networking events to attract new members. Use these free events to grow your visibility and to even find opportunities. Check with your local Chambers of Commerce and Small Business Development offices for networking events as well. When you attend these organizational networking events, market yourself. Have business cards ready but not just any business cards, quality ones. I used Vista Print when I got started and they are good for just that, starting out. It's time to upgrade. After all, do you want to get your card design from someone else?

You don't have to be afraid of the networking circuit. Most networking events are for business owners, like you, who are looking for connections and business exposure. Understand that not every networking event will be free. Some you will have to pay for. But research their alignment with where you want your business to go and then invest in the opportunity. Regardless of what you do, you need to network because you just might be able to connect with a mentor.

Finding a Mentor

At one time I thought having a mentor was a waste of time until I kept getting into situations that left me drained. I couldn't figure out why or how I kept finding the wrong clients, business partners and so-called opportunities. Then I realized, just like I need Jesus to call on and God to guide me, I needed a mentor to help me develop my business. So I looked to one of my mentors for my writing career, Thurman Jones, publisher of The North Dallas Gazette, a local community newspaper in the Dallas areas. Jones is one of the most intelligent men I have ever met. His advice is sound and he has a 'don't waste my time and I won't waste yours' mentality that we all need to start having. He is always willing to impart his wisdom into those who are willing to receive. And I go to him when I need to hear honesty about my missteps.

So my advice to you is to seek out a mentor or get advice from people who are where you want to be. Every business owner should have a mentor or two, who will encourage and challenge them as they grow their business. Being mentored or even coached is particularly good for those just starting out. It's not even a bad idea to have a mentor if you've had a business for a while. Just get with someone to give you direction when you need it.

Here is my caution … don't get a coach who isn't doing what you're doing unless they are your spiritual advisor. Matter of fact, that should be your first mentor or coach, Jesus. Take everything to Him first. Remember in the first chapter I talked about being frustrated? Well, that frustration can be reduced if you pray about your endeavors, clients and everything else first before moving forward. After talking to Him know that your earthly coach should be someone who is in the trenches of business ownership or has been in the trenches. If they have a 9-5 job and they can only coach you on their breaks or after work hours, then you may want to reconsider them as your coach. They only give good advice but they don't know what it takes to fully own and operate a business. They don't really understand sacrifice because they have a safety net called a paycheck that you don't have the luxury of having. So be cautious of these people because their advice can cause you to have slow to no growth.

Slow to No Growth

I had a client once who has had her business for over five years, that's the time most people say businesses either fail or start to succeed. Well she wasn't succeeding. Instead she was stagnant. She failed to invest in herself, in her business and most of the times she failed to believe in both. Having experienced so many people just like her, I decided to write an article called, *Small businesses are plagued by stagnation* in 2011:

> Oftentimes it is not the position of the financial
> markets which cause entrepreneurs to experience periods of
> stagnation or failure but rather the practices of the business

owner. Too many times I have encountered entrepreneurs who outright refuse to listen and apply business advice from other experienced and successful business owners. These failed and stagnated entrepreneurs typically become afraid or fearful of reports from the media, listen to nonprofessional individuals, such as a family or close friend or fail to make the right deals for their small business.

It becomes troublesome as a business consultant to continually render advice or submit detailed proposals to assist these entrepreneurs with understanding how they are hurting their business and limiting its full potential. Classic stagnation issues I have particularly witnessed and addressed with clients over the years include:

Refusing sound business advice. Former clients, who no longer have their businesses, outright refused to listen to the researched and proven data I collected because of their fear or listening to the advice of their friend or aunts who had a bad dream. They take the wrong advice and run with it. I usually hear back from them or find out that they started a new business.

Refusal to update business needs. Cheap is not a good business practice for a business owner and neither is spending money on unnecessary ventures or items. Entrepreneurs need to be savvy with their business dollars and find the best deals at the appropriate time.

Having the wrong people on board. Business owners hold on to unproductive employees because of concern for the well-being of the employee rather than the well-being of the company.

Not knowing market changes. Somewhat of a pet peeve is a business owner who does know or understand their market. They fail to understand when and how to move the company forward and at what times.

Business stagnation is the fault of the business owner and their unwillingness to use professional advice and sound judgment to keep their company thriving in any climate. Regardless of an economic climate a well-positioned business will thrive.

Again, it never seems to amaze me how so many business owners ignore advice from people who have experienced what they are trying to do. I mean I get it that presentation means everything to some people, but they miss the message. Think of it this way … if a homeless person told you to watch out for the cars that turn the corner too fast, would you listen? The answer that most people would say is no because he doesn't know what he's talking about. But think of it like this, he lives on that corner and knows the ins and outs of that corner, so you need to listen to him before you become road kill.

You have to get past your own self-image of what you think a business person is supposed to look or talk like. I mean would you honestly take advice from the suit and tie guy who lives in the Midwest about surfing or the dude who lives on the beach with a surf board, shorts and sandals on who looks like he's headed for the water? If you answered the suit and tie, you have more to learn than I thought and you need therapy to change your thinking. I would listen to Lil Wayne or Drake in a heartbeat because they understand what it takes to be a mogul. Despite not listening to their music I believe each of these men possess characteristics and know how to grow a business. Regardless of how they look, take heed because they are trendsetters in their industry.

Be a Trendsetter, Not Just a Follower

I know it may seem like I am beating a horse but it's for a purpose because you honestly need to know what it takes to be in business for yourself. In just the past couple of years alone, more businesses have closed down, while others are steadily cropping up. Everyone has or is facing some kind of financial hardship, especially business owners. Just making ends meet is no longer an option for the survival of your business. You have to do more with less.

Today, business owners are searching for new business trends to help them stay afloat. These business trends have sustained even the smallest business. Having multiple streams of income seems like a no brainer but for some business owners this concept is farfetched. Trends like micro-borrowing, online ad sales, direct selling, social media lead generation and freelancing are now a first choice for growing multiple revenue streams.

One trend to help you grow your business is called micro-borrowing. Like micro-lending, micro-borrowing is a new business trend that allows entrepreneurs to take out small lines of credit, typically under $5,000, for expenses or purchases. These microloans, as they are called, are required to be paid back in a shorter timeframe and require some form of collateral but they definitely help with the right now things. Micro-lending institutions are not traditional banks, therefore, the credit scoring or credit requirements are different. These institutions do, however, work with some established financial institutions to assist with establishing business credit.

Another trend to help business owners is online ad selling via your website. This opportunity generates residual online income through online ad placement and sales. Companies like Google and Yahoo! offer affiliate programs for businesses. To be a part of these company's affiliate programs you have to place various ads on your website or blog for a small percentage of revenue. Each time a visitor on your website click a sponsored ad, you receive a commission. You just have to make sure you abide to the rules and not click on your own ads. Commissions for online ad sales can reach well into the six figures but can be taxing to shift through and monitor.

The direct selling industry is more than 120 years old and companies like Avon help individuals generate additional income through the selling or distribution of their products or services. People who participate in direct selling have experienced moderate to high level of successes through part- or full-time work. Direct selling is becoming a popular trend for business owners who are looking to generate additional revenue. If managed properly, then this trend can become self-sustaining.

Another lucrative trend is freelancing. Many freelancers work short-term contracts within their industry. These short-term contract opportunities have become attractive to business owners because they can maintain the operations of their business while generating additional revenue. As a freelancer, you can create endless opportunities for your business by lending your advice or talents to companies who need short-term employees. I freelance with companies from time to time to hone my skills or make new connections.

As business trends come and go, you have to make sure you select the trend that doesn't detract from your business. While all business trends enable you to maintain and grown your business, you have to remember it is still a trend. Riding a trend past your immediate needs could become extremely costly in the long run. So stay abreast of your industry and the overall reason why you need to implement a trend into your business model. Each of these trends will definitely help you with advertising your business in some form.

Advertising is Essential

Another reason why business owners fail is because they absolutely refuse to advertise. They believe in Facebook, Instagram and Twitter. Guess what? These are just advertising and promotional tools. They are not the cure all to be all. When it comes to advertising, it's a known fact that your friends on Facebook and followers on Twitter will always support you. You can like and re-tweet without ever reading the details. It happens because I've done it. But when it comes to the actual supporters, your social media buddies may not show up. The number of bandwagon fans and followers never amaze me because when The BLI Group had its official launch in January 2013, the number of people on our Facebook page was staggering. So much so, that we reconsidered our venue, but God told us to be still and I'm glad we listened because out of the 200 RSVPs, only 50 people showed up. It was still a great event with great performances but still we could have spent an absurd amount of money if we went by the numbers from Facebook.

Trying to get business owners to promote their business through other media platforms, such as a magazine or newspaper ad, is hard work. They never see the value, so in my frustration I wrote, *Why advertising is important to entrepreneurs?*:

> Advertise here, advertise there. We got a deal for you if you just advertise with us. Being a small business owner means everyone has a way for you to advertise your product or service affordably or so it seems until you read the fine print. It is my belief that one of the hardest challenges for a small business owner is finding and selecting the right advertising avenue to use when promoting. Unfortunately some small entrepreneurs give up on establishing an effective advertising strategy thus failing to reach their full potential.
>
> You must understand the why behind advertising in order to find the right advertising avenue for your small business.
>
> Why advertise? Advertising by business standards is the ability to effectively develop a series of strategies which will inform and lure customers into your establishment to buy your product or pay for your service. But why is it important? Advertising is important simply because it is one of the most popular means to attract short- and long-term customers.
>
> Why can't I just use word of mouth? While word of mouth is one of the oldest and most effective methods of advertising it still comes at a price. The cost is operating your business day-to-day and paying your employees or vendors. You see you are still paying for a free service but it

should not be the only advertising you use. Be aware that word of mouth is a double edged sword and can be good or bad for your business.

Why do I have to spend money to advertise? Why do you have to operate your small business? To make money and advertising assists you with just that…making money. In order to make money you have to spend money. I am not saying rush out and spend thousands of dollars to advertise but what I am saying is that you should consider allocating at least 5-10 percent of your annual revenue to develop a sound advertising plan.

You don't need the fanfare of Superbowl advertising but you should at least have a plan which is catered to your business and works for your business needs.

It's sad how many people want something for nothing. They want your services or products but don't want to pay for it. Their excessive need to grow their business at your expense is endless and it's that kind of thinking that hurts the growth of business owners. They refuse to invest the necessary dollars needed to advertise their business. They think it's ok to get by with what they've been doing … nothing. They fail to understand that advertising doesn't have to cost millions of dollars, it just has to be strategic. One way of being strategic is street team marketing, that's having some quality flyers or posters made and going out to an event or even the mall and passing them out. It's time consuming yes, but well worth it.

Another way to advertise your business is through the small publications and media outlets in your area. These entities have affordable advertising rates. Unfortunately, the return can be slow because advertising takes time. It's like investing in the stock market, sometimes you can hit it big and other times you have to wait for a return on your investment. Just know that you need to invest in advertising, consistently, and to your budget.

Get Your MIND Right To Grow

Let's honestly look at what you are doing about strategically growing your business. Answer these questions and really take a look at how you think about the growth of your business.

1. What plans do I have for my business in the next 12 months, 3 years, 5 years or 10 years?
2. What are the current business trends in my industry or other industries that can help my company grow?
3. What is my advertising budget for each quarter and for the year?
4. Do I really understand the importance of advertising or am I always looking for a hookup?
5. How many networking events do I plan on attending for each quarter?
      a. Are they worth attending?
      b. Do I have marketing materials ready for these events?
6. Do I have a mentor in my industry who I can look to for advice?
7. Do I have an educational plan for increasing my knowledge about my business and industry?
8. What do I do to stay relevant? Is it paying off? How?

Chapter Six

Must Have Documents

Stop for a minute and ask yourself this one question ... what is the mission and vision of my company? I'll wait because I just may have stumped you. It's ok, this time. Many business owners fail to create a sound vision and mission statement for their business. They just know that they want to make money, be number one, or whatever trivial thought they have. But the large successful corporations have a clear mission and vision for their company. So why don't you?

Let me break it down a little better with one of my articles, *Conveying the mission and vision of your company:*

As a small business owner the one thing you should have on hand is a business plan which includes the vision and mission of your organization. The mission statement is the incremental goals of the organization and can be changed as needed to fit the development of the company. The vision statement is how the owner envisions the company in the future. Both statements set the direction of the company.

If you do not have a mission and vision statement or have lost track of what the true purpose of your business is, then here are some tips on how to effectively convey your company's vision and mission.

Create a vision statement for the overall purpose of the company. Never develop your vision statement to the current situation but rather what and where you envision the company being in years to come.

Create a mission statement that shows growth. Your mission statement is similar to the actions in an action plan.

It must be to the point but detailed enough for others to understand your mission.

Create a buy-in strategy for employees, customers and investors. A buy-in strategy allows your team, internal and external, to have a sense of ownership in making the company the best it can be.

Proudly display your statements. On every outbound communication tool you use should include the mission of your company.

Update your statements as needed. Your company will go through changes, big or small, so it is important for you to update your mission and vision statements to address those changes.

Without vision there is no hope, without a mission there is no change. Your business should have a clear mission and vision statement to display to the world that you are sure of the talents your business has to offer.

Change is inevitable and you know that as a business owner, change is one of the things you want your business to experience. You have to experience some degree of change, albeit positive or negative, for you to understand the impact your business is having. When you think of the change your business must go through, you need to have quantifiable data. Your business experience should align closely to your business plan.

Wait! Don't run! Let me finish helping you understand how simple a business plan really is.

Business Plan

You knew when you started your business that you needed a business plan. You need one to effectively establish objectives for how you plan to grow your business. It helps you identify the strengths, weaknesses, opportunities and threats your business will face and how to improve in those areas. Your business plan also helps you maintain and alter your path, when needed.

New business owners fail to understand the significance of evaluating and creating a business plan. The simple fact is that your business plan guides you. A business plan is the most important resource tool that you need to have created because it tracks the development and growth of your business. Don't believe that a business plan is important? Then think of all of the times your business grew in sales, employees or even experienced a loss. What did you use to measure those changes? Did you even have a plan to understand those changes? How did you plan for the next cycle of changes for your business? Not sure? Then you may now understand why a business plan is important.

Let's break down the components of a business plan:

- Executive Summary – Gives a brief overview of what the business plan will talk about. In the executive summary you should talk about who you are, what your business offers and how you plan to grow your business. The summary is an introduction of your business.

- Company Analysis – Allows you to give a strategic overview of your company. It also describes how you plan to organize your company. The company analysis is important for investors to read, so they are able to better assess if your business is worth their money.

- Industry Overview – Helps investors understand how you plan to position your business within your chosen industry and how your business fits into that particular industry. Industry overview primarily functions as a forecasting tool to help you predict any changes to the industry that may occur through trends.

- Customer Overview – Identifies the customers you plan to target. The customer overview helps you better understand which customers will patronize your business, what your target demographic of customers is, if your business will sustain a solid customer base.

- Competition Overview – This section will help you identify your direct and indirect competitors. This is an important section because too many businesses fail to work diligently to identify competition, large and small. In this section you will answer the who, what, why and how of your competition and how you plan to adjust to any changes.

All of these components work together to make sure you are able to strategically plan your actions, even when you are unsure of your next course of action. Some business plans also include marketing/advertising strategies, financial projections and forecasts section. All of these sections properly predict the future of your business.

Bottom Line – You need a business plan. You may have been successful navigating the through the storms and successes of business without one but you can achieve much more, including investor funding, if you just knuckle down and develop a sound business plan. Start with the Small Business Administration for help on how to write a business plan. Heck, there is even software available for writing business plans. Just create one or update your existing one.

Creative Ideas for Your Business Plan

If you don't know where to start with your business plan, never fear because I wrote an article about how to get creative with business plan creation called, *Get creative with business plan planning:*

The business plan is the key to the success and direction of any business. However, many entrepreneurs either fail to develop a business plan which will ensure rapid growth, prepare the owner for slow periods or a total change in the direction of the business. A traditional business plan is fine to create but being creative within the business plan opens up more possibilities for the business owner.

First, develop a basic business plan which includes a detailed explanation of the business; an analysis of competitors for the market being entered; details about the price, promotional strategy (marketing plan), placement for the product or service; and a summary with resumes of employees. This basic business plan will also include how any requested money will be repaid and how the initial business will be funded or financed.

Second, begin adding information regarding how the company will plan for steady or rapid growth. While the market cannot be predicted, financers want to know entrepreneurs are confident in their abilities to understand how to effectively plan for slow and rapid growth periods. Understanding how to express the ability to adapt to changes will help the business owner and the investor rest easier.

Third, explain any trends which are included in the business plan. Trends are not a usual addition to a business plan because of frequent changes but if the product is considered trendy then it should be explained to investors. The goal of explaining trends in a business plan is to show investors that the product will maximize sales goals and objectives during certain times of the year.

Fourth, show how nontraditional promotional concepts will work. This is one of the most out of the box thinking method for a business plan. With the use of social networking websites and inexpensive promotional companies available to entrepreneurs the use of these opportunities will show investors how strategically business opportunities can be planned. Social networking websites have enabled traditional companies the ability to reach clients in markets they would not have dared to venture into. The key to addressing social networking websites is to express how the pages will be used for business only.

Finally, updating the business plan is more than just a one-time event. Many entrepreneurs update their business plan when they are seeking additional funding. However, to have a business plan which is effective the plan should be updated yearly with any projected or made changes. The reason for updating frequently is to show investors the commitment to ensuring the business remains on track through the year.

Business plans are the foundation of the business but in order for entrepreneurs to be successful they have to find ways to think outside of the traditional business plan by adding creative solutions for the what-ifs and could be moments.

Advertising/Marketing Plan

The next important document you need for your business is the ever present marketing/advertising plan. This is a plan on how you plan to effectively tell your target audience about your business. Let me tell you this, if you have an entire proposal dedicated to using social media and you aren't a social media based company, then go dip your head in a dirty toilet and flush that stinking thinking. Seems harsh I know but come on let's be real ... social media is a tool, not the cure to your business advertising needs.

You need to advertise and market your business. An advertising and marketing plan consists of the following sections to help you and investors identify how you plan to capture your market. Here are the sections:

❖ Mission Statement. Your mission statement positions your company.

❖ Identify products and/or services. You need to know what you are going to sell or what services you are going to offer. Yes you can do both just be sure to clearly explain what they are, their ingredients and benefits.

❖ The market. You need to know the people who are going to purchase from your business. You can't exist thinking you know what it's going to take to get into a market so do the necessary market research before adding services or products.

❖ Competition. Who are your competitors? If you don't know or think you don't have any, then you just invented something that has never been invented. And that I seriously doubt. We all have competitors so be sure to know who yours are.

❖ Pricing. I have been guilty of not setting firm prices. But my single advice to you... don't do it. Set your prices from the beginning and only offer discounts when necessary.

❖ Promotion mix. What are you going to do to get your business exposed? Your promotion mix includes sales, discounts, and other promotions to attract customers. This is also where most companies place their social media push. Just be sure not to make this whole section about social media.

❖ Advertising. How are you going to advertise? You need to have an advertising budget because without it you are sure to sudden doom, unless you are niched. In this section you need to address your advertising budget and schedule, marketing and some promotional action items.

❖ Location, location, location. Do you need a storefront? If so where are you going to be located? If not, then how do you plan to operate your business? Figure it out and put it into words.

❖ Sales Forecasting. Do you know how to forecast your industry and its trends? When you deal with forecasting it helps that you set your prices then plan for promotions. My advice is to use an accountant.

❖ Action Plan. What action steps do you have in place to grow your business? This section is to outline how you plan to get where you want to go.

Every business owner runs into the wall of trying to figure out how to generate additional advertising opportunities. Everyone wants to advertise their business but no one wants to pay the price to advertise. Instead business owners spend countless hours on social media sites trying to add friends and followers in hopes of finding business in the mull of people who just want friend adds.

So how can you try to drum up additional business without spending excessive money? The answer is not as simple as it seems, but with a lot of effort you should be able to generate some business from these sources:

- Advertise in school yearbooks and local community based programs. I know this sounds pointless but these are simple and affordable ways to advertise your business. It is also reaching a market that you may not have considered. I used my oldest son's Jack and Jill of America Dallas Chapter Beautillion souvenir program book to advertise my business. The BLI Group purchased a full page ad for $200 and we were able to place our company in front of high dollar decision makers. Talk about a good investment. Advertising like this is a permanent opportunity for years to come, or as long as you stay in business.

- Sponsor a local event or youth sports team. This is a great way to get your business name out there. It also shows people that you support the community and children. People who sponsor events or teams potentially position their business to be seen by thousands, depending on the size of the event or organization's reach. If you can't financially commit to being a sponsor, consider exchanging products or services.

You'd be surprise what may be needed that your company offers.

- Send press releases to the local media. You need a good media kit regardless of the business you own. Send your press release to the various media outlets, large and most importantly smaller ones. In case you didn't know a press release gives notice to the community you live in about your business.

These are just a few inexpensive and less traveled ways to advertise your business. You don't have to spend thousands of dollars on advertising but you do have to spend some money to increase your exposure. Just be smart about how you plan to market and advertise your business.

Action Plan

With anything in life you need a plan of action. A daily plan of action is just as important as your business and marketing plans. You need to know where you are going on a daily basis and how you will accomplish those things strategically. Regardless of what you are planning you need to make a plan of action and set milestones in order to stay on track for reaching your goals. Unfortunately, making a plan of action and setting milestones aren't done and in business this can be detrimental to your company's growth.

The purpose of a making an action plan is to identify how a project will be completed and who the tasks will be assigned to, if applicable. On the other hand, setting milestones monitors your progress and ensure you stay on track. These two essential eliminates allow for the project manager to work through issues and properly identify best practices.

Even if you're a tenured business owner, you still need to understand how to define, measure, analyze, improve and control your business. In project management it's called the DMAIC Framework. This framework is perceived as the fundamentals of Six Sigma Lean and assists project managers with defining a plan of action and milestones. But for the purpose of growing your business we will only look at what's essential to business development and growth and how to create a tailor made Action Plan.

Let's look at 10 strategies for making an action plan and setting milestones:

1. Understand why you're going into business. You should perform due diligence to understand your industry, your tolerance as a business owner and your ability to grow your business. You should know if competitors have a similar business and how your business can be the best. Competitive analysis helps you understand your strengths and improve your weaknesses.
2. Define your mission and vision statements. A business owner without a mission or a vision statement is literally wasting time and energy. To be effective you must clearly define the mission and vision of your business so you can visualize where your business is going.
3. Know who you are. Every good business owner understands their strengths, weaknesses, opportunities and threats (SWOT Analysis). So to be effective, you have to come to grips with what you may or may not be able to do. Just ask you who you are.
4. Commit to your business. It doesn't matter if you are the most talented person known to business, if you're aren't committed to your business, then you won't be successful. So commit or go get a job.

5. Create the plan of action and set milestones. Now that you understand your competition; you have a clear vision and mission for your business; you've committed; you know who you are; you're ready to create a plan of action. Remember the plan of action and setting milestones helps you identify what you can do and what others can do for you. Your plan of action and setting milestones must be realistic.

6. Measure your progress. Measuring your progress is important. The way to measure where you are from where you need to be is as simple as writing it down. You will have the opportunity to identify measurement goals as you create this plan. Helps you understand and create best practices.

7. Perform an analysis. It's best to perform an analysis on your business. Analyzing your business should help you if you've been successful or not. Typically milestones aid as markers for performing analysis.

8. Improve where needed. Again once your milestones are developed the improvement process is easier to create. In the improvement stage you learn what challenges you had that impeded the development of your business. You need to learn from it and improve.

9. Control your business and the decisions you make. The control phase is also considered a milestone. The control phase allows you to ensure there are no issues that have gone unchecked. In order to establish control you must understand where you are. This allows you to determine if you have reached a business milestone.

10. Evaluate and recognize achievements. You will have a lot of successes in your business. With that you have to take the time to evaluate what you are doing as a business owner, preferably at each milestone, and then recognize your achievements. This establishes a sense of

success for you. Evaluating and recognizing, both milestones help with forward progress.

Owning a business is not difficult, especially if you get your head out of the clouds. Create a plan of action and set milestones because even the best laid plans can crumble. Remember these 10 strategies to help you create a plan of action and set milestones for the growth of your business. So there you have it. You have your business plan, marketing plan, action plan, now you need to have a branding plan for your business.

Branding Plan

Branding is essential. It identifies you before anyone ever meets you. Your appearance in public is a part of your brand. You conversation, conduct and character are a part of your brand. Things like your logo, website, and other marketing materials are a part of your brand. They all identify your business and establish brand loyalty. It's ok to change things once you get started but you need to start out by having a solid brand plan to avoid unnecessary changes in the future.

I wrote an article to help my readers understand the importance of branding:

> When understanding branding it is first and foremost important to understand what branding is. According to Vincent Grimaldi de Puget, a brand strategist at Grifin Partners, branding is the blend of art and science that manages associations between a brand and memories in the mind of the brand's audience. In other words branding is completed once a brand is established and the need for marketing, advertising and promotions are established. But what does it mean for a business owner with a business, idea, concept or product in a new market? These entrepreneurs face the challenge of branding in emerging markets.

Before concepts are identified for effective branding strategies for new and emerging markets, the core components of branding must be identified. These core competencies if you will are:

The *brand* is the product, service, business or even you that you want to establish a presence with. Think about it this way, the things you buy and use every day are brands, regardless of their popularity or not.

The *attributes* are those things that make the product, service worth buying or using. On the other hand, value is the worth to the buyer. You may have that one thing you can't live without, that's your perceived value of that product.

Finally, there is *brand management*, which is what your company is doing to effectively manage the messages, marketing, advertising and promotions of your business.

Now that you know the fundamentals of branding, let's look at what an emerging market is. An emerging market is a new or up and coming market that is untapped. Emerging markets can become a silent killer to businesses market research is not conducted. Yes, even companies with a popular brand carelessly enter into markets without researching it, thus losing millions.

Going Into New Markets

There's opportunities in dem dere hills. Well, not really in the hills but there are new markets for you to expand into, even within your local market. Most of the business owners that I talk to want to have affluent clients but don't want to leave out of their current market. You have to be ready by having your mind right and your business must be up to par to enter into that market. Now, if you want to go into a new market for clients, then fear not I have some advice on that as well.

First, research the market you are considering entering. Going after clients in new markets cab be challenging especially if your business is not prepared for demand and supply. Take the time to research the market and what products or services should be entered in it. Stop having the mentality that everyone is going to want your product or service. Trust me, as successful as McDonalds is, not everyone wants to eat a Big MAC. And if people reject them, then you don't stand a chance with that way of thinking.

Have you ever noticed how a product or service can be in one market but not in another one? Well that's because of market testing. Test your product or service through focus groups, surveys or samples at local vendor opportunities. Lay's Potato Chips is notorious for market testing. They test their new products based on market research and regional preferences. A cardinal rule to remember is that people like what they like. So be one of those businesses that research to give the people what they want or need.

You need to understand how you're going to brand your business as well as how you are going to track what's working and what's not working. Picking your brand management campaign is essential when going into new markets. A good brand management plan deters losses. To go further into brand management, you need to use all advertising mediums available to you. These mediums include:

- Social media provides great brand management planning to add to your branding plan for new markets. You can announce your debut through these mediums, raise awareness or invite consumers to buy.
- Networking. There's that word again. But it's important with increasing brand awareness. Networking allows you to find opportunities that are more cost effective while providing you with the same reach. Networking opportunities are plentiful in new markets and help establish a strong brand.
- Spread the word by sending emails; getting into local

media outlets; or by street team efforts or hitting the streets. Your only focus should be giving the people something positive to talk about.

- Contrary to popular belief the press is not only interested in reporting bad news, so reach out to every media outlet in the new market, be sure to be specific to your industry, and tell your story. Invite them out and if they don't show, keep trying.

Branding in new markets is only difficult when market research is not conducted. If you are targeting a new market, then it is beneficial to the success of your business to research if your service/product will be needed or wanted. Develop a brand management campaign to ensure your business' success. Get the word out through social media, traditional media, networking and word of mouth. Tackle a new market by strategic placement, not wishful thinking.

To further help you understand branding let me say this, you are sadly mistaken if you think that your brand is your logo only. Your logo is just one aspect of your brand. You need to make sure that you build your brand holistically. Promising something to a customer, even if it's a phone call builds brand trust. Having a service or product that people enjoy builds brand loyalty. All of these plus the visual aspects of your company helps build your brand.

Now, what else do I need to talk about … oh yes, your paperwork. Do you have that in order or are you just flying by the seat of your pants, making changes as things come your way?

Paperwork Plan

Whenever you start anything that requires money to be exchanged you should have a contract that details what is being rendered and what the amount you expect to collect. Unfortunately, for me and others, we get a new client, they screw us over all because we failed to get a contract in place. You need to always protect yourself from shady business people.

Contracts

Business contracts are a must have for any business but there are business owners who still don't have these essential documents in place. Contracts are designed for one purpose – to protect the interest of all vested parties. When you have a contract in place, you have a legally binding document that is enforceable in a court of law. Even verbal contracts can be upheld in court. The trick with having a contract in place is knowing what to put in it to protect your business from fraudulent business owners who willingly sign contracts with no intent of making good on it.

When writing out a contract you should get a lawyer to review your contracts to make sure that your business is protected. You can also use LegalZoom.com for lawyer reviewed contracts and other legal documents.

"Having a contract in place does two things," says Mario Clark, Contract Manager at The Rane Agency, "It protects you and it protects the person signing the contract. The problem comes when people sign a contract and don't understand or list the necessary things to protect themselves in case they default on the contract."

Defaulted contracts occur all the time, rather intentionally or not. When someone defaults on a contract, then the contract goes into default. Default can be refusal to uphold the contract specifications, refusal or inability to pay and several other requirements including legal and collection measures.

Oh and on another, don't let folks out of contracts because

they have a sob story. I was notorious from letting people out of their contract. One of my former clients capitalized on my desires to help her out. When it came time to pay, she had a sob story and I gave in. After two retracted contracts I realized she was hustling me. So enforce your contracts.

Policies and Procedures

Everywhere you go there are policies and procedures that you must adhere to. If you return an unwanted item to the store, then there is a policy and procedure for that. If you have your car worked on at the dealership, then there is a policy and procedure for that. You get the point? Policies and procedures are needed to maintain order for your business.

Unfortunately, too many companies fail to establish clear policies and procedures for their business and then they get upset when things go haywire. Cut all that foolishness out and list out the rules of engagement for your business. Clearly define how you handle customer disputes, employee issues, nonpayment, contract disputes and enforcements, delivery of services or products, and other regularly occurring issues.

Employees

When you being hiring employees you documentation specifically related to employees. Just think about the paperwork you received when you got your first real job. There may have been an employee handbook, an application, W-4 or I-9 form, job responsibilities and rules, breaks, time calendar, benefits handbook and other documents. The company you worked for clearly outlined who you were to them and what they were to you… your employer. You may not need all of the documents you had but you need roles and responsibilities, an application, wages, and an employee handbook to make sure your employees understand where they stand with your company.

Contractors

Hiring a contractor requires an understanding that they are not your regular employee. They usually only works for a set timeframe or for a specific project. When you hire a contractor you need a contractor's agreement or subcontractor agreement that clearly defines the action items like scope of work, payments, disputes and other issues related to their job.

Proposals

Remember the episode of The Cosby Show where Vanessa brought Dabness, her fiancée, home for a dinner? She didn't tell Claire and Heathcliff beforehand about her dinner guest and when Heathcliff finally got a chance to talk to Dabness, he related their introduction to a steak with all the trimmings being brought to the table on a garbage lid. I say all of that to say, your proposals are the first impression of your business. So be sure that it meets and exceeds the expectations of the bid you are submitting for.

A one page proposal won't cut it. You need to have details about the scope of work (at least what you plan to do), who you are as a business, who the key players are, your cost, the hours associated with completing the project, and other things that they list in the Request For Proposal or RFP. Be as detailed as possible until you feel comfortable about making your point. And please do a grammar check.

Media/Press Kits

Regardless of the type of business you have you still need a media/press kit. These kits shows the exposure that your business has received. It is also useful when you're trying to get additional media coverage or advertising opportunities. What's in a media kit is simple you need previous press coverage, a list of products with pricing (pricing is optional), what your company is about and a press release. Those are the simple forms of a media kit. They do get detailed but should not be more than 10 pages and definitely shouldn't be wordy.

Other Necessary Documentation

There are wealth of other documents that you need for your business. These documents may include a DBA and other licenses, state sales tax licenses, bank accounts, certifications, collection letters, clients and employees notices, vendor applications ... just a lot of paperwork for just in case moments. Start with Google to find the right paperwork for your industry.

Get Your Foundation Right

It's time to answer serious questions about the foundation of your business. Answer these questions and really take a look at what you have done so far to protect your business from different dangers and position it for new opportunities.

1. Do I have a sound business plan in place? If not, do I know where to begin to get one created?
2. What does my marketing plan look like and is it right for my business?
3. How do I handle disputes and other issues within my company?
4. What are my policies and procedures are they relevant to my customers, industry and legal?
5. Do I have a media or press kit from my interviews and exposure to the public?
6. What kind of proposals do I send out? If I received the kind of proposal I send out would I hire that person?
7. Do I have contracts in place that protect me and my business or do I shake hands and hope for the best?
8. Do I have all of the necessary paperwork completed or updated for my business? What are they? Are they current? If not, then why?

Chapter Seven

More Tips

I think I have talked enough. It's time to wrap this book up, so in this chapter I am just going to give you some more get your mind right tips for your business. I have included a few more of my published articles for you to read. You can always go to Examiner.com and search for me or you can do a Google search. Yes, I am Googlable (That's my word).

Effectively planning your work day

As a business owner it may seem that your work is never complete. You wake up running to catch up and go to sleep feeling like you are behind. And during the day, everything seems never ending. So how can you get your work day organized and work smarter not harder? Simple … plan. You should never go through a day without being properly prepared. Here are some tips for effectively planning your work day.

Create a list of sorts to organize your thoughts. Some people prefer checklists, while others like to do lists to make it through their work day. Regardless of the list you choose to get through your day you need to create on. You can use the traditional notebook method so you can write down what steps you took or what follow-up you need to do or you can do it all from your smartphone. The goal of a list is to get things accomplished and track your progress.

Manage your time. One of the things many entrepreneurs fail to do effectively is manage their time. They may spend hours on social media sites updating profiles or just wasting time all together. Not saying being on social media sites is a waste of time but it should be limited and managed. You must realize that as a business owner your time is valuable and spending hours on things that do not significantly impact the growth of your business could eventually detrimental.

Delegate if you can. Yes, you have to wear multiple hats as a business owner but do you have to do everything yourself? No, you can delegate. There are resources available for entrepreneurs including volunteers, interns and part-timers who are looking to either gain experience or earn some extra cash. If you work on a contract basis then set a smaller contract pay scale or hourly wage for the extra help you need. Don't be greedy and try to keep all of the money yourself that you are pulled in a million ways.

Make necessary calls and return necessary emails promptly. Follow-up is the name of the game for many businesses, especially if you are a service business. Unfortunately, entrepreneurs fail to respond to emails and phones calls because their day is compacted with tasks or things that are not necessary to growing their business. With that set a time out of your day to make phone calls and return emails. Hopefully you are making phone calls and not subjecting your email to SPAM.

Get rid of the unnecessary clutter and mundane routines. Fitness is great, but if you are not a personal trainer then you don't need to schedule your work out sessions during your work day unless you have downtime. Catching up with your friends is awesome but unless you are a life coach or counselor, catching up should only be done after hours. If you have an office and there are unopened packages, then open those packages and shred documents you don't need.

If you don't take your business serious, then neither will anyone else. You can't expect to grow a successful business living and working in chaos. Get organized and prioritize your day. Here is a scripture to remember to get to the business of running a business – Proverbs 10:4-5 *"A slack hand causes poverty, but a hand of the diligent makes rich. He who gathers in summer is a prudent son, but he who sleeps in harvest is a son who brings shame."*

Wasteful habits of a small business owner

The last thing a you need to do is waste your time with unnecessary and unproductive tasks which takes the focus off of the real reason they are in business. To make money. Unfortunately, many entrepreneurs hurt their businesses by developing wasteful habits which yield no substantial rewards for the benefit of the owner or the company.

Some of the wasteful habits that entrepreneurs have including myself are as follow:

Internet usage. Internet usage can be both productive and counterproductive if you are visiting websites which are not business oriented. If you are using social media sites then get on and do what you need to do and get off. No need to be liking someone's shoes or tweeting the latest gossip, unless that's what your business specializes in.

Making unnecessary purchases. I know you have a need certain for certain inventories, supplies and advertising needs to remain viable but ask yourself do you need it right now. At that very moment. I admit it, I am a compulsive buyer at times so before I get to the cash register I ask myself do I need what I am getting right now. This is not to be confused with running low and then making the assessment but honestly thinking if I need something or if I am just being compulsive. Unnecessary purchases that can be used for personal needs hurt the bottom line of your business. So be wiser about your purchases.

Micromanaging. If there are tasks which need to be specifically monitored until they are complete, then get to it. Other than get off folks back and let them do the job you hired them to do. This is why I tell you to check those around you because if you have to be a micromanager because you can't trust anyone then you need a new team. Or you are a control freak in which you still need to get your mind right.

Playing referee. When you own a small business or are an entrepreneur doesn't it seem like you always have to play referee? Everyone calls you to handle problems but guess what? That's not your sole job as an entrepreneur trying to grow a business. Again, in the previous chapter I talked about your team and if you have a team that is always fighting and wanting to put you in the middle then you are wasting time and money. You should not have to babysit grown folks. It's that simple. Either they get their mind right or they need to get away from you.

Meeting just to meet. Not all business meetings will yield the outcome needed, to sign a contract. So don't waste your time driving to and from just to meet with someone. Your business meetings need to be productive and have an outcome. Don't be afraid to ask those questions when someone asks for a meeting. If they want to know your services then tell them over the phone or in an email but definitely don't waste your time chasing behind them. Stop wasting countless hours attending meeting which yield your company nothing.

Continually offering free services. Once people find out that you are passionate about what you do they will more than likely attempt to siphon information from you. I have been a victim of this countless times. I use to just talk and talk and talk and they would take all the information and never use my services. I mean in the 15 years I have been an entrepreneur I can honestly say that I have given away about a $1 million in free advice. Yep I said a million because my hourly rate is $125. If you talk to everyone about potential business, then you undoubtedly hurt your ability to retain clients and make a profit. So SHUT UP!

Wasteful habits are hard to break but for the success of your business, you need to understand to always think of the mission and vision of your company first. Then you need to determine if what you are doing is helping or hurting your business. Finally, just SHUT UP and stop talking to everyone unless they are ready to sign on the dotted line.

Managing your time

You have to manage your time as you manage the other functions of your business. With the day-to-day issues you encounter it's easy to become unorganized. And once you become unorganized you ruin your professional image, client's trust and growth. You should never go to client meeting unprepared, talk to someone without knowing the specs of what you have to offer then, but lacking knowing and being unprepared happens when you are all over the place. So get it together.

Understand that first and foremost your time is valuable. You will be pulled in various directions leaving you to feel like you are running in circles. Unfortunately your business cannot afford endless laps around an imaginary track. To manage your time use a calendar either on your computer (Microsoft Outlook or Email), cell phone (yes your cell phone has a calendar feature), or a planner (a good back-up).

Track your expenses in the simplest form or until you are able to afford accounting software. There is never a good reason for you to lose your receipts, forget to collect on payments or not know the balance of a bill. To stay on track financially, use a computer based spreadsheet (Microsoft Excel), an analysis pad (located in an office supply store) or a lined notebook.

Keep your personal and business email separate. Starting out in business you may not understand the value of having more than one email address until you are sifting through countless junk mail from friends and emails which do not generate potential client leads. Having at least three emails, one for personal, one for sales, and one for inquiries, can assist you with managing the emails your receive and track viable leads.

Your time is valuable, your money is important and determining leads from junk mail are a few key organizational tips for the small business owner.

Bartering services

Bartering is an age old trading system between at least two people who are in need of or want for the other's person's item. For instance, if someone is in need of a service or product you may offer and you are in need of a product of service they offer then an exchange would be the ideal framework for both parties. Many business owners understand that in order to get something for their business that they need they need to collectively bargain and barter with other business.

As with any systems and structures in business there are some advantages and disadvantages of bartering.

The advantages are:

1. Receiving the services or products you want or need for little to no cost.
2. Building a systematic bargaining chain to use when needed.
3. Possibly no contractual obligations – meaning there are no unfair commitment requirements.

There are many more advantages but the disadvantages should be readily identified as well:

1. Bartering services can consume your time and work schedule to negotiate the deal that works best for all parties.
2. Bartering can become tedious.
3. You may not have an equal trade for what you need or want. Meaning if you are willing to barter a $1,500 service or product and the person you are bartering with has less than that in product or service then the trade becomes unequal.

So how do you establish an effective bartering system or network to get what you need or want? This is an answer that is not easily formulated because you have to have willing participants. Next, you have to ensure that the products and services are what you want and need. Bartering just because is not ideal for any business. If you locate business owners who are willing to participate in the bartering network then you have to ensure that everyone can contribute equally. Finally, never abuse the bartering system for personal gain. Bartering is just one way to establish an effective network of small business owners.

Chapter Eight

Resources

I couldn't leave before I gave you some great resources to help you propel your business into the next stratosphere. In this final section, seriously this time, I'm going to give you websites, letter samples and other things I know are important to growing your business.

Request for Proposal

A Request for Proposal is typically written when work needs to be completed from an outside vendor or by another department internally. The RFP should describe the project, the response you are looking from vendors, the steps in reviewing the proposal including a timeline and pertinent contact information.

It is important when writing the RFP that a pool of vendors, or potential bidders, are selected and notified. You can submit a notice in your local newspaper, online or media source to let bidders know of the project or you can be very selective in your approach and reach out to preferred bidders. With either notification method you should consider writing a Letter of Notice for the RFP.

Most letters are similar to this particular letter:

Date
Individual's Name
Company Name (if applicable)
Street Address
City, State and ZIP

Salutations
Body of letter should include an introduction, give a brief description of the project and have contact information for interested parties. A deadline to respond for interest should also be included.

Close the letter with your name and title.

Once you have your bidders identified you should begin writing your RFP, which is more detailed than the Letter of Notice.

Here is an example of a Request for Proposal outline:
- Executive summary
- Statement of need
- Project description
- Organization information
- Project schedule
- Budget
- Conclusion

Now here are a few examples of Request for Proposals:
Company Name
Company Address
Company City, State and ZIP
Company Phone

Project Name Request for Proposal

Introduction
This section should be an introduction of the company, the team and the project.

Overall Project Goals
This section highlights what the company finds to be the ultimate goal of the project, the end results. Vendors should answer in their bid how they will make the project goals feasible.

Scope of Work
The scope of work details the project and how the company will work with the vendor to ensure completion.

Requested Information and Proposal Format
This section is to address how the requested information and proposal format should be submitted. In this section vendors should meet and/or exceed the needs of the projects when they return their bids. You should not be willing to compromise on what you expect to receive back from the vendors.

Optional Services
This section addresses any additional services that may be required from the vendor.

Ownership and Intellectual Property
This section explicitly expresses the ownership of the project and all intellectual properties. Vendors may be willing to give you what they create for you but may not be willing to give what they created and used for the creation of your project, such as software, programs and the like.

117

Company Responsibilities

This section highlights the responsibilities of the company to ensure the vendor receives all documents, schedules and other pertinent information to stay on track with the success of the project.

Estimated Project Duration

This section gives an outline of the timeline from the RFP response submission date to the final decision date. Make sure you allow time for changes and alterations to the project and RFP.

Submission Information

This section helps the vendor with how to submit their bid and what the requirements are.

Selection Criteria

This section helps the vendor understand the selection criteria, so be sure to include your contact information for bids and questions.

Miscellaneous

This includes any additional comments or services required by the company to the vendor.

Not all RFPs are written to include these items. RFPs can and should be altered to fit the immediate need of the department and project.

Here is an example of a Request for Proposal to help you write a detailed RFP:

    o Cover Letter
    o Signature Page
    o Title Page
    o Table of Contents
    o Schedule of Events

o Standard Terms and Conditions
o Special Terms and Conditions
o General Information
o Definitions
o Purpose or Intent
o Background
o Method of Payment
o Contract Term
o Presentations or Demonstrations
o Pre-Proposal Conference
o Technical Specifications
o Specifications (Goods)
o Scope of Work (Services)
o Scope of Activity
o Project Management
o Deliverables/Measurable Standards Schedule
o Support
o Training
o Maintenance
o Vendor Requirements
o Mandatory Requirements
o Vendor Organization
o Vendor Qualifications & Experience
o References
o Financials
o Resumes
o Proposal Response Format
o Cost Proposal
o Method of Evaluation & Award
o Evaluation Criteria
o Discussions, Best & Final Offer
o Negotiations
o Attachments

Collection Notices

[**Your Name**]
[**Street Address**]
[**City, ST ZIP Code**]
July 2, 2012

[**Recipient Name**]
[**Title**]
[**Company Name**]
[**Street Address**]
[**City, ST ZIP Code**]

Dear [**Recipient Name**]:

Is there some reason you have not paid your bill of $[**amount**]?

Your signed service agreement states that you agree to pay this bill in [**number of payments**] installments. Your [**payment number**] payment is now overdue by [**number**] days.

Please remit payment of $[**amount**] by [**date**]. If you have any questions or concerns regarding this bill, please contact me at [**phone number**].

Failure to send the full amount by [**date**] may mean that your account is turned over to a collection agency. Your prompt attention is required to resolve this issue.

Sincerely,

[**Your Name**]
[**Title**]

Contractor Agreements

The Subcontract Agreement (the "Agreement") is made and effective with the conditions hereafter expressed on this _____ day of _____, 20____

BETWEEN:

_____ (the

Contractor)

AND:

_____ (the

Subcontractor)

Whereas Contractor has entered into, or will hereafter enter into a public relations contract henceforth "The Prime Contract" with

_____

to perform in accordance with various contract documents and specifications certain work prepared by

_____ to create, develop, monitor, execute and deliver a (explain services here) for

_____(the Project) on

_____.

Whereas Contractor desires to retain Subcontractor to perform certain contract work in accordance with various contract documents and specifications and/or to furnish labor, materials, supplies, labor and/or goods for The Project.

Now THEREFORE Contractor and Subcontractor agree as follows:

SUBCONTRACTOR WORK

Subcontractor shall be employed as an independent contractor and shall provide and furnish all labor, materials, tools, supplies, equipment, services, facilities, supervision and administration necessary for the proper and complete performance and experience of the following portions of the work, hereinafter "the Subcontract Work", for the Project, together with such other portions of the Project as related thereto:

SCOPE OF WORK: (Insert Text Here).

TIME OF COMPLETION
   a) The Subcontractor will provide the Contractor a schedule of completion of deliverables for the Project no later than

   _____.
   b) The Subcontractor agrees to adhere to the schedule and understands failure to do so could result in this Subcontract being cancelled and payments nullified immediately.
   c) The Subcontractor shall employ persons of competence and skill to assist with Project as needed. The Work shall commence by _____.
   d) If the Subcontractor fails to complete the Work as agreed herein, the Contractor may declare the Subcontractor in default by providing written notice to Subcontractor by registered mail. If Subcontractor fails to remedy such within fifteen (15) days of such notice, Contractor shall have the right to select a substitute Subcontractor. If the expense of completing the Work exceeds the unpaid balance on this Contract, the Subcontractor shall pay the difference to the Contractor.
   e) In agreeing to complete the Work by the agreed Time of Completion, Subcontractor has taken into consideration and made allowance for ordinary delays, and hindrances incident

to such Work, whether growing out of delays of common carriers, delays in securing material or workers, changes, omissions, alterations, or otherwise.

SUBCONTRACTOR PRICE

In consideration of Subcontractor's performance of this Subcontract, and at the times and subject to the terms and conditions hereinafter set forth, Contractor shall pay to Subcontractor the total sum of $_____$, hereinafter "subcontractor price." Said subcontractor price is dependent upon the conditions set forth in Scope of Work being met. Should said conditions not be met, the subcontract amount shall be modified accordingly.

1) The Subcontractor shall, on his time and expense, submit to the Contractor a release of all material liens and manufacturer warranty and materials information for all materials used prior to final payment.
2) Final payment, constituting the entire unpaid balance of the Contract Sum, shall be made by the Contractor to the Subcontractor when the Contract has been fully performed by the Subcontractor and when and only when final payment is received from the Project.
3) Such final payment shall be made not more than thirty (30) days after approval by Contractor and receipt of final approval by the Project.
4) Subcontractor may make application for progress payments to the Contractor each month. All requests received by the 20th day of the month will be paid by the 15th day of the following month. Those requests received after the 20th day of the month will be considered part of the following month requests.
5) At no time is the subcontractor or its employees allowed to file Workers Compensation or file suit against the Contractor or Project for injuries or incidents.

6) Subcontractor understands that the Contractor is not responsible for filing taxes, local, state or federal on behalf of the Subcontractor.

7) Contractor is not responsible for paying or compensating employees hired or volunteers working with Subcontractor.

8) Subcontractor agrees to pay for any damages, misrepresentations or falsifications created by the Subcontractor.

9) All requests for payment must include an original of the following:

    a) An invoice describing the Work that was performed;

    b) The payment amount requested; and

    c) The estimated of percentage of the Work completed.

SPECIAL CONDITIONS

The Special Conditions to Subcontract are incorporated in this Subcontractor as though fully set forth herein. Subcontractor hereby acknowledges receipt of Special Conditions.

COMMUNICATION AND NOTICE

a) All communications between Subcontractor and General Contractor, Client shall be via Contractor.

b) Subcontractor shall furnish Contractor with periodic progress reports as required by Contractor, including status of material, equipment, manpower and submittal.

c) Contractor and subcontractor shall use all necessary methods of communications and contact which include email, phone or in person meetings. All communications should be done within the Contractors hours of operations which are Monday – Friday 8:00 a.m. to 6:00 p.m. Any communication after this time shall be deemed emergency.

d) Subcontractor agrees to not text any Client or Project related inquiries to Contractor.

RIGHTS

Subcontractor agrees that at no time are any materials, mechanics, thoughts, ideas, concepts or the like as related to the Project are the property of the Subcontractor. Contractor retains all rights, usage and reproduction in conjunction with the Project. Subcontractor may use approved portions of the Project for portfolio only building purposes and any use must acknowledge the Contractor.

NON COMPETE DISCLOSURE

For good consideration and as an inducement for Contractor to subcontract with the Subcontractor, the undersigned Subcontractor hereby agrees not to directly or indirectly compete with the business of the Contractor and its successors and assigns during the period of employment and for a period of one year following ending or termination of subcontracting and notwithstanding the cause or reason for termination.

The term "not compete" as used herein shall mean that the Subcontractor shall not solicit or consult the Client or Project in which the Contractor may substantially engage during the term of subcontracting.

CONFIDENTIALITY

The Subcontractor acknowledges that the Contractor shall or may in reliance of this agreement provide Subcontractor access to trade secrets, customers and other confidential data and good will. Subcontractor agrees to retain said information as confidential and not to use said information on his or her own behalf or disclose same to any third party.

AMENDMENT

This Subcontract shall only be amended or modified by written

125

document executed by authorized representatives of Contractor and Subcontractor. This Subcontract supersedes all prior representations made by Contractor.

ARBITRATION

Any and all disputes or claims between the Contractor and Subcontractor arising out of this Subcontract shall be resolved by submission of the same to an attorney, for resolution by binding arbitration according to the Rules of Arbitration. In so agreeing the parties expressly waive their right to a jury trial, if any on these issues and further agree that the award of the arbitrators shall be final and binding upon them as though rendered by a court of law and shall be enforceable in any court having jurisdiction over the same.

This agreement shall be binding upon and inure to the benefit of the parties, their successors, assigns, and personal representatives.

_____   _____
Signature   Date

_____   _____
Signature   Date

Press Releases

Diabetic Innovator Announces New Injection Aid

SOUTHAMPTON, Mass., Nov. 1, 20xx — When faced with the certainty of daily insulin injections, innovator Chris Hillios knew he had to design a device that would help him overcome his injection anxiety. Through his determination and innovative spirit, Confidisc(TM) was developed.

Confidisc is an aid for injecting, by syringe or pen, insulin or like medications. It can be used by the patient or by a caregiver. "It is truly amazing that a simple device like Confidisc can make such a huge difference in one's life. Our testing has shown that Confidisc not only reduced pain perception, it clearly reduced injection anxiety," said Chris Hillios. "Users focus on the disk rather than the needle." With Confidisc's help, patients' lab results are now better than ever.

Confidisc enables users access to a larger range of injection sites, allowing better injection rotation. It provides added stability in both filling the syringe and during injection. It's simple form is easy to use, convenient and cost-effective. Confidisc may be manufactured as a reusable attachment product and/or as a permanently fixed part of a hypodermic syringe. As a new hypodermic syringe, Confidisc also helps to deter illegal intravenous drug use.

More than 18 million Americans are living with type 2 diabetes. Many suffer from injection anxiety. Fear of injection can lead to improper treatment and poor control.

"Having first-hand knowledge of the problems associated with home injections, it is our belief that this product will be of enormous benefit to the ever-growing diabetic population. Confidisc provides the confidence I need. I will no longer inject without it," said Hillios.

Confidisc was well-received by a review of Endocrinologist, Diabetic Educators and Nurse Practitioners. They look forward to having it available for their patients. It is sure to be a beneficial, simple, and affordable product for everyone facing daily injections.

"Diabetes was our primary concern. However, we can now see that as the self-injectable market grows, the uses for Confidisc also grow," said Hillios.
PHOTOS AVAILABLE

Contact:

Chris Hillios
P.O. Box 90
Southampton, MA 01073
Phone: 413-527-4059
http://www.confidisc.com
info@confidisc.com

# # #

DISCLAIMER: This press release was taken from The BIG Press Release Samples Book Press Releases for Every Occasion and Industry by the editors at eReleases.com & Press-Release-Writing.com.

Service Agreement

Date

Client Name
Business Name
Address
City, State, ZIP
Phone
Email

Dear Client Name:

This proposal is being prepared because I am positive that fostering a working relationship will be beneficial to establishing your brand and positioning you (Enter Company Name) to become (List client needs). I have created a list of services you will receive for the agreed upon (Enter Amount) for services through (Enter Date). After that time we will reevaluate and reassess your needs and associated fees.

AGREEMENT
(Client Name) and (Your Company Name) agrees to begin services for (list services/products being rendered). The fee is (Insert Cost) for services through (Enter Date), beginning (Enter Date), not including (Insert dates). Client agrees to provide The Company with all the necessary information within 48 hours of request. Failure to provide requested information may result in a delay in work and production. Company agrees to meet with Client once (Enter location details) for work to be completed as well as in person or via the phone. Any other work will be worked offsite at a location determined by Company. It is understood that Company will provide services for Client on an assignment basis. Our normal fee does not include (list what your fees

do not include). The following services include:

- List services of agreement

This branding opportunity will position Company to become (List client goals). Once we have satisfied we will revisit this agreement and assess other opportunities for Client.

TERMS

All payments are due on the (Enter Payment Date). Invoices will have a (Enter Payment Terms). A nonrefundable deposit of (Enter Payment Amount) is due at contract signing. Remaining payments are due (Enter Dates) in the amount of (Enter Amount).

Work will not be delivered or continued until all balances are paid and current.

Meetings, attended events and hours worked are considered billable hours. All minutes, 0-59, are billed as an hour by the Company. Any hours not worked will not be carried over. The Company will provide hourly invoices to the

Client prior to payment being submitted for tracking and record keeping purposes. Failure to pay invoices will result in a (enter amount) late fee of the entire balance. Continued failure to pay balance could result in collection or legal efforts being pursued by The Company.

All work must be approved by The Client unless otherwise noted. All documents and design work will receive three (3) revisions. Revisions must be requested within 72 hours upon receipt. Failure to approve or request revision within 72 hours of receipt by The Client will cost (Enter Amount) per revision request. All revisions will be made by

The Company within 48 hours.

This contractual agreement will expire on (Enter Date). Any and all projects not completed by agreed upon deadlines will be charged normal applicable service fees, to be determined by the Company original rate price.

Client and the Company will identity obtainable goals via a calendar for the Company to achieve. Any goals that are unreasonable, including short timeframes, unrealistic expectations or the like will not be agreed to. The expectation is to deliver a streamlined and consistent brand message for all departments to use including but not limited to the sales/marketing team.

It is the expectation of the Company that Client and her appointed officers will maintain an open line of communication including emails, phone calls, meetings, and text messages. Failure to do so could result in delayed deliverables.

If you agree to these terms and the services set forth in this letter, then please return this letter with your signature and date.

Signature	Date
Signature	Date
Signature	Date

Helpful Websites

Resources
http://www.WomenCeo.com
http://www.SBA.gov
http://www.DNB.com

Documentation
http://www.Netapp.com
http://www.Officearrow.com
http://www.RFPservicesonline.com
http://www.Webcrawler.com
http://www.irs.gov

Press Releases
http://www.web-press-release.com
http://www.prsync.com/submit-press-release
http://www.indiaprwire.com
http://www.adagepressrelease.com
http://www.press-network.com
http://www.pressreleasepedia.com

Branding
http://www.thebligroupllc.com

ABOUT THE AUTHOR

Ivy N. McQuain is a seasoned professional writer, PR consultant and business strategist. Whatever our clients need is always done and done in excellence. She has a BS in Marketing from Southern University in Baton Rouge, LA and a MBA from the University of Phoenix. Ivy has been writing and consulting since 1998.

She started her first business at 19 when she was a fulltime college student at Texas Southern University in Houston, TX She has extensive experience with building companies in their local markets through written communications.

Ivy formerly owned Written By INC and Organized Noise PR Consultancy but is now the managing partner of The BLI Group, a multimedia services firm specializing in branding. Her partnership with publications, businesses and individuals has garnered her as an expert in the communications industry.

A native of Kansas City, KS, she now resides in the Dallas area and is the proud member of the Inspiring Body of Christ Church under the leadership of Pastor Rickie G. Rush in Dallas, TX. She is also the proud mother of teen sons, Demerial C., 17 and Nickohlas J., 13.